COLLECTING ROYAL HAEGER

A Comprehensive Illustrated Price Guide
* Highlighting the Figurines of the 30s & 40s *

by
Lee Garmon and Doris Frizzell

Photos by Jay Barnard

COLLECTOR BOOKS
A Division of Schroeder Publishing Co., Inc.

The current values in this book should be used only as a guide. They are not intended to set prices, which vary from one section of the country to another. Auction prices as well as dealer prices vary greatly and are affected by condition as well as demand. Neither the Author nor the Publisher assumes responsibility for any losses that might be incurred as a result of consulting this guide.

This Book is Dedicated to . . .

the men and women, both past and present, who made . . . and continue to make . . . Royal Haeger possible!

Acknowledgments and Appreciation

A very special thanks to The Haeger Potteries, Inc., their facilities, and their personnel: Alexandra Haeger Estes, President; Joseph F. Estes, Chairman of the Board, and Nevina Zarbock, Advertising Director and Librarian - gave so much of their time and memories; Susan M. Campbell, Secretary to Joseph F. Estes, and our liaison in this adventure.

Jo Cunningham, for pointing us in the right direction

Betty Latty Hurlburt for support in our venture.

Betty Carson of Betty's Collectibles.

Neila M. Bredehoft, for Heisey Collectors of America.

Ruth B. Hickman, widow of Royal A. Hickman.

Hope Hickman Hamilton, and husband, Harvey Hamilton.

Dennis Stanek, President, A.L. Randall Company.

Medley Distributing Company for Ezra Brooks.

Gould/Burkart Collection of Houston, Texas, for sharing.

Our wonderful friends for bringing unusual pieces of Royal Haeger,
    and our families, who understood and helped make this happen!

Table of Contents

Introduction

A look at today's market would reveal a vast assortment of collectibles - ranging from pottery to glassware; from primitives and breweriana to railroad china and World's Fair memorabilia; and from old fishing lures to optical items - anything and everything from A to Z. We collectors are well organized, and boast books on every conceivable subject.

As the collecting field is so diversified, let us concern ourselves here with pottery only (American made). In the world of pottery collectibles, there are such names as Hull, Roseville, Hall, McCoy, Shawnee, Weller, Stangl, Frankoma, Red Wing, Van Briggle, Rookwood - only to mention a "few." There are books and articles galore on each company, but an Illustrated Identification and Price Guide for collecting Royal Haeger is long overdue. The *demand* is there, and the *need* is there . . . the need to preserve this legacy!

The Haeger Potteries, Inc., having been in business these past 117 years, is vastly important to our American clay heritage. We are excited by Royal Haeger, and know our "fellow collectors" share this pleasure.

The main thrust and focal point of this guide is directed toward the prestigious Royal Haeger line, and its dramatic design interpretations. Initially, Mr. Royal Arden Hickman was the Chief Designer of the Royal Haeger line, launched in 1938.

Although our primary concentration will be on the 12 year period following the introduction of Royal Haeger, we have "spilled over" in some areas - for the benefit of the collector. While trying to separate the past from the present, our research turned up information in other categories we felt was vital to the reader. Wherever possible, we have relayed these findings.

Invitation to Our Readers

Although Haeger philosophy is one of "look ahead" - collectors are definitely "looking back" - back to the 30s and 40s - back to the dynamic designs and glazes of the Royal Haeger line, its lovely figurines and accessory pieces.

We have done a great deal of research to verify the facts presented here. We have toured the Haeger plants and Museum; we have visited with Joseph F. Estes, Chairman of Haeger's Board; we have interviewed available personnel from Haeger's past; we have been in correspondence with Royal Hickman's widow and daughter; and we have contacted a great many dealers from different areas. Our experience in collecting Royal Haeger is quite extensive, as is our collection!

Now, and it is with great pleasure and pride, we offer our comprehensive Guide for collecting Royal Haeger. This book has something for everyone, and represents a sincere and honest effort on the writer's part to bring organization, as well as a starting point, for this collectible.

More specifically, this Guide is designed to serve a three-fold purpose:

1. For those inquiring about Haeger's early beginnings, it will offer a brief history of the family Haeger, through the four generations;

2. For those interested in the life of the gifted designer, Royal Arden Hickman, it will provide a view of his background and accomplishments; and

3. For those collectors and dealers of Royal Haeger, this Guide will serve to identify, describe, illustrate, and catalog numerous pieces from this line, as well as the Studio Haeger and Royal Garden lines. Also offered, will be information on "reasonable market prices" as gathered in our travels and research.

As we find no evidence of any other Collectors' Guide being established for Royal Haeger, we consider ourselves "trailblazers" in this endeavor. As collectors, we realize that first efforts, no matter how thorough, cannot include every piece out there. HENCE . . . the invitation to our readers for their input, such as: descriptions of additional pieces, photos, labels, colors, prices, numbers . . . anything and everything not included in this Guide. We look forward to hearing from other collectors. The author can be reached at: 1529 Whittier Street, Springfield, Illinois 62704 (SASE).

When an author writes the initial book establishing a "new" collectible, letters pour in with more and different information. And, a couple of years later, Volume II is written. We hope for this, we want our readers to participate!

We have a good feeling about Royal Haeger, and everywhere we go, the vibes are the same - someone is always asking about it. This pottery generates excitement, and suddenly, one finds themselves "hooked on Haeger"

Prologue

Beyond the feeling that it is "convenient" to drink our tea or coffee from a pretty cup, to beautify a niche or corner with a graceful vase, or to light a lamp tastefully placed at our elbow, do we give thought to the objects, shaped from clay, that grace our everyday life?

How do they come into being? What has inspired them? How are they created?

The art of the potter is the oldest in history. Art was born when man first sensed his need of tools for cutting and scraping. These early tools he fashioned from stone. From almost the beginning of time, man has made and used pottery.

The caveman carried clay into his retreat, and with the crude implements made from stone, along with bits of wood, he first made vessels and utensils. He worked with clay before he knew metal. He patterned some of his earliest receptacles after the skin and leather bottles in which he carried water.

Primitive and pre-historic man; potters in the ancient lands of the Nile; Mesopotamia (where tradition places the Garden of Eden); Assyria; ancient Egypt; Cyprus; Greece; China; modern Europe and Japan; and in the ancient and modern Americas, for countless ages, man has made his contribution to art, its use and beauty (dedicating it at times to their gods or to their sacred dead).

Practically every continent and island in the world has had its beds of clay. The necessary tools of the potter are few. Everywhere, and at all times, the story of the making of pottery has been essentially the same: there was a need for vessels; there was clay from which they might be created; there was fire to burn them for hardening; and, as always, man's desire to satisfy his enduring quest for beauty.

Ancient commerce carried its great pots of oil from port-to-port. Ancient races made pottery their medium of barter. Ancient tombs have yielded up all manner of utensils and the inscribed tablets - complete libraries of them - from which the modern scholars and archeologists are still revealing the history of the earliest civilizations.

Many centuries ago, business wrote its bills-of-lading on clay tablets and baked them. They kept their books upon them, sent their invoices baked in clay, and such early tablets became the fore-runners of the modern check.

Because of this widespread prevalence of clay and the simplicity of the tools required, every race and age has known the art of the potter. At times, several of them discovered and developed it simultaneously, each without the knowledge of the other, although there is a direct descendency of such discoveries that may be traced from pre-historic times down to the present day.

Literature Knows the Potter

Literature has universally celebrated the potter's craft. The poet Keats has immortalized the lovely Grecian urn in his inimitable ode: "Omar". The English poet Browning, in his "Rabbi Ben Ezra" regards mankind as the symbol of the "Consummate cup" molded by the potter god. He bids us to note the rapid spinning of the potter's wheel and seize the moment here at hand to live!

Dickens has left us his bit of fiction: "The Plated Article", a record of his visit to the Spode factories. Arnold Bennett will make the potteries of northern England live forever in his novel "Clayhanger" (and its sequels). The English writer, Priestley, took a try at the potter's wheel in this industrial district, and was inspired to write the fascinating commentary in which he philosophizes about the skills and intricacies of the art.

In Mythology

Going back a great deal farther, we find Greek mythology crediting Vulcan with the creation of the first woman, Pandora, out of clay. Later, Keramos, the son of Bacchus and Ariadne, became the patron saint of the potter. It is from his name that we derive the term "ceramics" or "keramics" - that branch of chemistry and the allied sciences which are devoted to the making of pottery and the kindred industrial arts.

Again, in Egyptian mythology we read how Ptah, or Num, the creator of the world and the first potter, took clay of the Nile in the cradle of civilization, turned it on his wheel and made man, breathing into him the breath of life. In Hebraic literature, especially in the Bible, we come upon a host of allusions to man, the clay and Jehovah, the potter, who made man "of dust of the ground", while in the New Testament, we are told of Jesus working miracles with clay. In every other literature and mythology we find this same symbolism.

What is Pottery?

In its simplest form, pottery is "the shaping or molding of a piece of clay into a useful or beautiful form and its hardening by heat".

Your reference books will give you various definitions, all reducing, however, to the broad meaning: everything made of clay and hardened by fire.

The humble earth-red drain tile, which was known to Roman engineers, the soft and mellow roof tiles of Spain and the other sunny Latin countries, share this definition, together with pre-historic inscribed tablets from ancient tombs; the precious Ming vases out of China; the coarse stoneware of early New England; the most fragile eggshell porcelain in the cabinet of the connoiseur from French or Austrian or Chinese potteries; the treasured American lustre; old Italian majolica; and countless other objects . . . made of clay and hardened by fire . .

Classifications of Pottery

We divide all pottery into three general classifications:

First, there is *earthenware*, the least expensive pottery, which differs primarily from the others in that body and glaze are made of the same material;

Secondly, there is *stoneware*, a medium grade of pottery, of which our jugs, jars, steins, and heavier grades of tableware are made; and

Thirdly, there is *porcelain*, the finest, most expensive grade of pottery. Down through generations the artisans and artists have wrought exquisite results in this medium, which we are accustomed to calling "china".

How Did Pottery Begin?

Civilization has progressed as man has become conscious of his needs and sought to satisfy them.

No one knows who first discovered that clay, when mixed with water, could easily be molded into shape and turned into a hard stonelike substance when exposed to fire. It is not known who first discovered that by dipping this porous pottery into a mixture of melted sands and other minerals, and firing it again, it could be given a glasslike impervious finish.

Somewhere, very early along the way of human life, it might have been when man first realized that fire could make the flesh of beast, bird, and fish more palatable, that he also realized his need for a fire-proof utensil. Then, he might have taken a gourd and covered it with clay to protect it from the fire, and in this manner, made his earliest experiments with pottery.

Again, observing how his sun-baked footprints in the clay along the bank of the stream, held the rain until it evaporated, he might have taken this for his pattern and created the shallow receptacle which he clumsily developed into a bowl or jar when he sensed that he could carry water or cook with it. Or perhaps the savage had his earliest inspiration from the nest which the birds lined with clay. He might have made his first mold by covering, the inside or outside of the baskets he fashioned from twigs and rushes with clay - like the birds wove their nests. He possibly took other patterns from cuplike plants.

Interesting, and altogether probable, are any or all of these speculations. Of them, and of others which have advanced down through time, we may take our choice. We do, however, know for fact, that close to 4,000 years before the Christian era, men were using both the potter's wheel and the kiln. On the temple walls in ancient Thebes, we may read in pictures, the complete story of pottery making with the two elements which join the ancient art to the present - fire and clay!

Primitive Pottery

Primitive pottery was hand-fashioned. It was baked in the sun or in the open fire, smoothed and welded while the clay was kept moist with water, and colored with natural earth pigments.

With a stone, a bone, or a stick - even with his teeth - the potter incised or embossed his designs which he took from the natural world about him, the plants, animals, even the rhythmic lines of waves, hills, and rivers.

His pottery was strictly utilitarian. He used it in both his domestic life and religious ceremonials. Ancient mounds and pre-historic ruins still reveal his primitive pottery.

Archaic Pottery

Archaic pottery, the products of the earliest civilizations, was wheel-fashioned and kiln-fired. As early as 3700 B.C., while the Egyptians were covering their clay with a heavy enamelling, the Chinese were working with the fine porcelains which have been the delight (and despair) of successive centuries of would-be imitators.

Egypt passed her art along to Persia. China gave her secrets to the ancient Hellenes. In Attica, between 700 and 200 B.C., we find these Greeks making pottery of a restrained and elegant beauty which has never been surpassed. In the world's museums and private collections, there are thousands of these ancient red and black Greek vases. These record for us, all that is known about Greek painting. They reveal the home life of the Attican, his recreations, his hunts and his battles.

This earlier Greece also knew the mixing-bowl and water pot, the storage jar and oil bottle, the pitcher and the drinking cup, as well as the vase.

At this time, ancient Rome was creating its sealing-wax red Samian ware, which precious secret was lost with the fall of Rome, to be re-discovered several centuries later by the Robbias.

In Persia, 300 years before the Christian era, we find the finest application of color to architecture that this world has known. We see famous specimens of this in the Louvre - life size friezes of human and animal figures in relief - of surpassing beauty and brilliance. Also, the Persians created a vivid and striking enamelled ware. Examples of this rare and choice art can be seen in the Paris Gallery.

Persia uniquely preserved a contribution to the potter's art in the hanging lamps of her mosques. Her vases and dishes were copied in Rhodes and the Levant. In the tenth century, when the Mediterranean world was linked with the Greek world, Egyptian design (the palmetto and the lotus) arrived to break up the geometric.

In the 12th century, Italy, France and Burgandy learned much about the making of pottery from the Saracens - previous to the influence of the Moors from Spain and Sicily.

These Moors, working with tin and lead in their experiments with glazes, developed an enamelled ware of great loveliness in simple color range with magnificent metallic lustre. Italy surpassed it with her majolica in its wondrous cobalt and rich lustres. Sumptuous ware of this character was made in the factories of the Medici in 15th and 16th century Florence.

Sienna, in northern Italy took her rich brown earth and made pottery. Venice produced her more delicate and fragile wares, Luca della Robbia incarnated, with an immortality, the Italian Rennaissance potteries with his garlanded terra cotta tiles and medallions. These wares boasted the loveliest of blues, soft as the Italian skies, as well as colored fruits, flowers and figures in relief.

Other Italian potters of this period adapted, in decoration, the great masterpiece paintings.

These potteries, and others of their period, belong largely to the earthenwares. Nine-tenths of the ware in museums as well as individual collections, is of this character.

The Modern Potters

We date the beginning of the modern world with the Rennaissance. In the course of this, the French, with their fine feeling for texture, line and color, became the master potters of Europe.

In the 14th century, Faenza Italy became the center of invention and experiment, and gave this name to all the faience - that is, the enamelled ware - of southern Europe. In the various countries, this differed only in its decorative treatment.

Bernard Palissy excelled with this ware in France. The faience of Rouen and Nevers, and other Centers, succeeded his in the 17th Century. In the 18th century, we begin to find enormous quantities of this ware adorned with bouquets and festoons of figures in colors. We also have the Dutch Delft of this same time period.

The Dutch have made important contributions to the potter's art. Dutch traders brought the Chinese porcelains into Europe as early as the 13th century. Europeans tried vainly to imitate them, taking for one thing, the suggestion of the blue Delft ware from the famous blue and white of the Chinese. A price was on the head of any Chinese who might reveal the secrets of these porcelains, which were protected by the government. Not until the beginning of the 18th century did any Europeans succeed in approaching it.

Then, however, we have Bottger, the alchemist, pondering one morning while he powdered his wig, wondering if the white powder he was using might not be effective in the making of porcelain. Sure enough, it worked! We then had the finest Dresden china and the secret of kaolin (or true porcelain) becoming known in France. Porcelain was being made at Saxony and Sevres, as well as Vienna and Berlin.

The secret of fine porcelain traveled from France to England. The use of bone ash in Cornwall, introduced bone china. Out of Ireland came the beautiful Belleek, fragile as an eggshell and exquisitely glazed.

In Northern Europe

In Northern Europe, Germany and the low countries were experimenting with stoneware at an early date, using the salt glaze (that the English potters inherited later). In subsequent time, this part of Europe - Germany and Austria in particular - developed pottery among their peasant arts.

In the earlier day, fine stonewares were made in Cologne, and elsewhere in the north during the 17th century. Also, during this time frame, Japan began to produce her famous yellowware, Kioto and Satsuma, nearer to stoneware than earthenware.

The English Porcelains

English potters earliest works were in coarse stoneware, making its butter pots, mugs for ale, and various jugs. At this time, the rich still set their tables with silver and pewter, while the poor used wooden ware so there was no demand for china.

The story of the English porcelains, however, is a highly interesting saga.

This begins with Josiah Wedgwood, who created his cream ware - or queensware - and his blue and white jasper with its fine classic bas-reliefs, as well as his basalt and crystalline with colored veins running through it between 1765 and 1810.

The first of the famous Wedgwoods, whose family has come down through the profession to the present day, made his first porcelain tableware for Queen Charlotte (wife of George III). Also, he made another service for Catherine of Russia. Josiah Wedgwood was the first to employ celebrated artists as designers and decorators.

Wedgwood was made a Fellow by the Royal Society, in tribute to his influence upon the entire subsequent course of china-making. His Portland vase became the most famous specimen of its sort in modern manufacturing.

Contemporary with this earliest Wedgwood, there was another famous Josiah among the first English potters - Josiah Spode. He, like Wedgwood, began his apprenticeship to the art in his childhood. His formula was original with him. His product still lives, having passed some years ago into the control of the Copelands.

Coalport and Minton, Lowestoft, Staffordshire and Worcester, Doulton and other English tableware and decorative pottery exemplifies, with Wedgwood and Spode, the finest specimens from the English kilns.

It is important to mention the delightful Chelsea figures and other baubles, inimitable in their beauty of modelling, which came out of England, and charmed every lover of the beautiful. The Bow potteries made a ware similar to Chelsea, and ranking high in delicacy. Lowestoft was an offset of Bow, but more imitative.

Napoleonic wars and the industrial revolution of the later 17th century, brought the break with the craftsman trade in every facet of its expression. The machine came to usurp the hand tradition, and commercial ware threatened to eclipse the hand-created ware entirely.

Our American Potters

Except for the primitive aboriginal Indian pottery, the

craft did not come to America until after the Revolution. Even then, so ingrained was the preference for English wares, that the earliest of the American manufacturers imprinted their wares with British trademarks.

Primitive pottery, however, yielded up from Indian mounds on the Atlantic coast, and in the Mississippi Valley, on the Pacific slope and elsewhere, is better studied in this country than anywhere else.

The making of post-Revolution pottery in New England and the south Atlantic coast states is another fascinating story. The Gruby, Dedham and Merrimac works and the popular Bennington wares, peddled by picturesque wagons through the country, gave the purveyors prestige as men of a genteel profession. Around New York, Trenton especially, and spreading to the Ohio country, the making of pottery followed interior settlements.

Pottery as a fine art received great impetus, as did art in its other expressions, from the World's Columbian Exposition in Chicago in 1893. Most exquisite specimens were brought from all over the world inspiring a more universal interest in such treasurers. Many of these lovely pieces remained in this country, housed in individual, museum, or private collections - increasing in value as time passes.

Main source of material for this Prologue—Irma Dupre, deceased, Dundee Town Historian.

A Brief History of Haeger

First Generation

On the banks of the Fox River in Dundee, Illinois, David H. Haeger began his brick yard in 1871. The river banks provided the clay for the bricks that helped rebuild Chicago following the Great Chicago Fire.

From this beginning, Haeger Potteries has progressed to its position today as a pacesetter in design and innovation. Haeger art pottery is found everywhere in the world where selective good taste is evident.

Tradition Began Here

David H. Haeger founder 1871.

Second Generation

Upon his death, one of David's sons, Edmund H. Haeger, assumed leadership of the Dundee brick factory. His early recognition of the value of brilliant color glazes and distinctive design, was responsible for the initial popularity of Haeger art pottery introduced in 1914.

Under Edmund's leadership, the organization was transformed from a conservative establishment - devoted exclusively to the manufacture of brick and tile - into the world's largest art pottery.

From the first piece of Haeger artware in 1914, the pottery utilized both lusterous gloss/glazes and soft glowing pastels - velvet to the touch. (We understand these early pieces were marked with a triangle shaped label). The glazes would include lovely deep roses, yellows, oxblood, and bronze with gold tones.

Dignity, distinctive design, and dramatic color were three of the main ingredients responsible for the continued popularity of Haeger pottery.

As a highlight in the 1934 Chicago World's Fair, Edmund built a complete working ceramic factory, showing both ancient and contemporary modes of production. This remarkable exhibition and the wares produced there, are more fully discussed following this brief Haeger history.

Edmund H. Haeger 1900-1954.

Tradition Continues

Figure 1. Commemorative Copy of Haeger's First Piece of Artware, Classic Greek Vase, 1914.

In 1971, Design #1 was reproduced for the 100th Anniversary of The Haeger Potteries, Inc. Highlighted in gold, this commemorative Classic Greek Vase was made in a limited edition, numbering 2,500 pieces. The mold was then destroyed. (The bottom of the vase bears the inscription: ''Haeger Centennial 1871-1971'').

Third Generation

Family leadership continued at Haeger with the appointment of son-in-law, Joseph F. Estes as general manager in 1938. Expansion and diversification have been the fruits of his guidance. The Royal Haeger line of artware and lamp bases he introduced is one of the most respected in the field. In 1938, he was instrumental in starting The Haeger Potteries of Macomb, Illinois. Located in an area rich in clay deposits, this plant produces a complete line of pottery for florists.

In 1954, Joseph F. Estes was named president of The Haeger Potteries, Inc. He became chairman of the board of Haeger Industries, Inc. in 1979.

Tradition Continues

Joseph F. Estes, 1935.

Fourth Generation

This generation of Haeger leaders is represented by a son, Nicholas Haeger Estes, and a daughter, Alexandra Haeger Estes, the great-granchildren of the founder, David H. Haeger.

Family leadership sustained the continuing growth and expansion of The Haeger Potteries, Inc.

In this year of 1988, the pottery is celebrating 117 years of creative craftsmanship . . . the winning combination is still winning . . . the Haeger name remains synonymous with good taste and sound business practices!

The need to diversify, and the rich clay deposits in central Illinois, prompted the opening of a second plant at Macomb in 1969. This plant, The Royal Haeger Lamp Company, is devoted entirely to the manufacture of lamp bases and shades. In 1979, Nicholas Haeger Estes, son of Joseph F. Estes, became president of this company.

Nicholas Haeger Estes

In 1979, Alexandra Haeger Estes, a daughter of Joseph F. Estes, was appointed president of The Haeger Potteries of Dundee. In February of 1984, Alexandra was elected president of The Haeger Potteries of Macomb. In June of the same year, she became president of Haeger Industries, Inc., Dundee, Illinois, and was elected to the Board of Directors.

Alexandra Haeger Estes

Edmund Haeger's decision to build a model "working" pottery exhibit at the 1934 Chicago World's Fair Century of Progress Exhibition, further introduced the Haeger line to Americans from every part of the country.

This modern exhibit included a large display of Haeger's wares, as well as a complete working factory. The pottery produced on this site was exhibited and sold in the adjacent showroom.

Modes of pottery production, both ancient and contemporary, were also included in the exhibits. As an interesting contrast to the working factory, Mr. Haeger employed Indian potters from New Mexico to demonstrate their primitive methods of making and firing their pottery.

A front porch ran the entire length of the Haeger Exhibit building. This porch, rustic and primitve in appearance, was specifically designed for Maria Montoya Martinez and her husband, Julian, to demonstrate their techniques. (Maria, now known the world over for her black pottery, was a member of the Tewa speaking Pueblo Indian Tribe). Every effort was made to duplicate the exact conditions under which Maria shaped and fired her "Maria Pottery" in San Ildefonso, New Mexico.

(In 1971, 36 years later, Maria would return to the Haeger Pottery in Dundee and present them with a magnificent black pot, in honor of their 100th anniversary.)

More than four million persons visited this educational exhibit and watched the making of Haeger pottery. Without realizing it, they were, in fact, watching history being made!

NOTE: The Haeger artware pieces completed during this "Century of Progress Exhibition" were so designated with paper labels, and sold only at the Fair. (See section on labels).

— 13 —

Summary of Milestones in Haeger's History

1871 - Founded by David H. Haeger (born in Mecklenburg, Germany in 1839).

1900 - Edmund H. Haeger, David's son, assumes leadership.

1914 - Haeger's first piece of artware (Classic Greek Vase - Design #1).

1934 - Worlds Fair Exhibit - a complete working pottery.

1938 - Joseph F. Estes, active in the firm since 1935, is named vice-president and general manager.

1938 - The prestigious Royal Haeger line was introduced! This dynamic concept with it's brilliant colors and unique handcrafted designs, was second to none . . . the magnificent Royal Haeger carved its niche in time, for all future generations.

1939 - The Royal Haeger Lamp Company is formed.

1939 - The Buckeye Pottery Building was purchased in Macomb, Illinois. This site was devoted exclusively to the manufacture of artware for the florist trade.

1946 - The pottery celebrates its 75th anniversary!

1947 - The Haeger Awards, a national ceramic design competition, was developed for this anniversary year.

1954 - Joseph F. Estes becomes president, upon the death of Edmund H. Haeger.

1969 - The Western Stoneware factory was purchased in Macomb, Illinois, becoming the new site for the Royal Haeger Lamp Company.

1971 - 100th Anniversary - "Craftsmen for a Century" . . . Few companies span a century . . that Haeger Pottery has not merely survived, but truly thrived, is a tribute to its leadership.

1979 - Joseph F. Estes becomes chairman of Haeger Board.

1979 - Nicholas Haeger Estes, Joseph's son, is president of The Royal Haeger Lamp Company.

1979 - Alexandra Haeger Estes, Joseph's daughter, is president of The Haeger Potteries of Dundee.

1984 - Alexandra Haeger Estes is president of The Haeger Potteries of Macomb, and of Haeger Industries.

1985 - Joseph F. Estes celebrates his 50th year as the "Man at Haeger's Helm".

1988 - The pottery celebrates 117 years of creative craftsmanship.

Haeger continues to maintain its position as leader in the field of ceramic production through careful management of its facilities; by streamling, mechanizing and automating wherever possible; by employing leading designers; and by staying in tune with the public moods and wants.

Figures 2, 3, and 4 represent progress made in mold filling: from hand-pouring, to pumping liquid slip through a hose, to the automatic mold filling operation.

Figure 2

Figure 3

Figure 4

Figure 5. Haeger's First Milk Bottle Kiln - 1916

Figure 6. Haeger's 1935 Facility at Dundee.

Figure 7. Haeger's Present-Day Facility at Dundee.

Designers Past & Present

The staff of Haeger can boast many fine designers during its history, many of whom learned their art in the great pottery centers of the Old World. Other designers from Copenhagen, Sweden, and Finland contributed their skills as well. These gentlemen, along with others listed below, were, and are, master stylists in their field. Out of their dreams and diligence, we have the proud products of The Haeger Potteries, Inc. today.

Haeger's famous glazes, frequently imitated, but never successfully copied, are made by expert craftsmen, requiring extensive training. The glaze covering a piece of pottery must be perfectly mixed and blended. It must be hard and durable when fired, but it must not break or crack. Above all, the color must be clear and lusterous. The dipping must be dextrously done to insure a uniform coating of the bisque. The possible shrinkage from firing must be estimated so that body and glaze will contract proportionately to avoid cracking or breaking.

Two men, Mr. Franz Joseph Koenig (deceased) and Mr. Robert Heiden (deceased), are noted for their contributions to Haeger glaze making and design engineering.

Mr. Koenig, born in Holland, studied art in Haarlem and was trained in the Royal Potteries of pre-war Germany, near Koblenz. In addition to Mr. Koenig's formal training and subsequent positions, he was sent by the Dutch government to the Dutch Indies in Africa for research and experimental work. This work was done with regard to the introduction of the potter's craft into these colonies.

However, in due time, America beckoned, and Mr. Koenig came to the Haeger Potteries for a long and successful career.

Mr. Robert Heiden started his career with the pottery in 1913. He knew every phase of Haeger's progress since he helped cast the first piece of artware produced by the pottery. Haeger relied upon Mr. Heiden's thorough knowledge of glaze making and firing when developing new glazes.

Others would include:

Martin J. Stangl, who left his employment as superintendent of the technical division of Fulper Potteries, Flemington, New Jersey, to help in the development of Haeger's artware line in 1914. Stangl's tenure with the Haeger Potteries lasted five years, at which time he returned to New Jersey to establish Stangl Pottery. *Important Note:* occasionally, a piece of Haeger will be seen signed by J. Stangl. These pieces are indeed a rare treasure for the collector!

Royal Arden Hickman, chief designer for the Royal Haeger line introduced in 1938, now deceased. (See page 21)

Eric Olsen, Norwegian artist, formerly associated with England's famed Wedgwood and Spode, retired after a 25 year tenure with Haeger. (See page 33 for a profile of this renowned artist/sculptor).

Edwin K. Kaelke, executive vice-president and general manager (deceased) also did some design suggestions.

Lee Secrist, art director (no longer with Haeger) headed the design group, anticipating trends and styles.

Martin I. Deutsch, New York sculptor and painter, made a number of significant design contributions.

Joseph Pfanzelter's Studio in Larchmont, New York, has been the origin of some Haeger pieces.

Maria Fuchs, in addition to deisgns in silver, metal, plastic, and glass, created new forms for Haeger-ware.

Elaine Douglas Carlock, designed sketches of her small sons, subsequently modeling them in clay, working from her farm near Cincinnati, Ohio. Also modeling children in clay, designer *Martie Strubel* created the ''Magical Moments'' line.

Helmut Bruchmann, important past ceramic engineer for Haeger, now deceased, innovated and created unique glazes and techniques.

Among Haeger's free-lance designers, we find the names of: Ben Seibel, top New York designer (now deceased); Sascha Brastoff; Lawrence Peabody; and Helen Conover, who did designs during Mr. Olsen's tenure, under the label of ''Studio Haeger''.

Presently with Haeger, *Alrun Osterberg Guest,* ceramic engineer, continues to oversee the beautiful glazes of this pottery, while *C. Glenn Richardson,* chief designer, continues in his dramatic design concepts. (See page 18 for profile).

Haeger maintains permanent showrooms in the following locations, introducing new lines twice a year:

Atlanta - Merchandise Mart
Bedford, Mass. - The Center
Columbus - Col. Gift Mart
Dallas - Dallas Trade Mart
San Francisco - The Gift Center
Northville, MI - Room B-40
Kansas City - Merchandise Mart
Denver - Denver Merchandise Mart
High Point - Southern Market Center
Los Angeles - LA Merchandise Mart
Minneapolis - UMAGA Gift Mart
New York City - New York Merc. Mart
Seattle, WA - 6100 Building
Reston, VA - Suite 301

C. Glenn Richardson
Director of Design

Growing up in a family of artists, Glenn took first place in a design competition at Lane Tech High School, resulting in a job offer from an art studio. He then went on to Wright Junior College and Illinois Institute of Design.

While serving in the United States Marines during the Korean War, he took advantage of courses in art and design at San Diego Junior College and did design and art work for Special Services of the Marine Corps.

In 1954, Glenn joined Plasto Lamp Manufacturing Company as head designer. He later opened his own design studio, and in 1968, accepted a partnership in Lite America Lamp Corporation.

Mr. Richardson has been designer and sculptor with The Haeger Industries, Inc. since 1971.

His design interpretation is unexcelled!

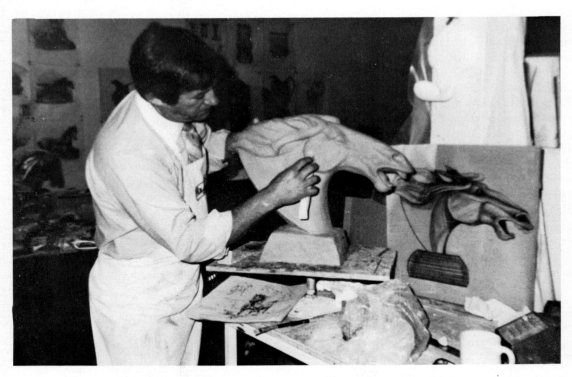

Mr. Richardson creating one of his magnificent designs.

4020-54-975   Ht 30"
Black opaque shade
54 Sandstone, 09 Porcelain White
Lucite mount and finial

4040-09-974   Ht 27"
Cream linen shade
09 Porcelain White, 54 Sandstone
Lucite mount and finial

4030-26-974   Ht 26"
Cream linen shade
26 Ebony, 09 Porcelain White
Lucite mount and finial

Sebastiano Maglio
Master Potter

Presently at The Haeger Potteries, Mr. Maglio "throws" on the Potter's Wheel, designing one-of-a-kind creations . . . offered exclusively by the pottery. Mr. Maglio holds the honor of being a seventh generation Sicilian potter.

The potter's wheel is a revolving disc with motive power supplied by the potter's hand, a foot treadle, or mechanical means. The lump of softened, kneaded clay is thrown upon the center of the disc, and as it spins, the potter with his strong, dextrous hands shapes the vase or bowl from inside and out.

The use of the wheel is almost a lost art. However, this ancient method, used by potters since the beginning of time, can, yet today, be witnessed daily at the Haeger Potteries.

Mr. Maglio indeed possesses the potter's thumb, as he lends himself to the feel of the clay. Effortlessly and with a smile on his face, his skilled hands continue to work their magic!

The fundamental principle of the potter's wheel, like that of the loom of the weaver, endures today - unchanged through all the ages.

Mr. Maglio, along with other Hager associates, is also credited with making the world's tallest art pottery vase. This vase, over eight feet tall, is listed in the 1983 Guinness Book of Records.

Shown below, is Alexandra Haeger Estes, president of Haeger Industries, and the magnificent art pottery vase.

Joseph Estes estimates between 650 and 675 lbs. of clay were used for this vase - finished in 1977. The painted scenes portraying potters at work were done by C. Glenn Richardson.

Royal Arden Hickman

Designer - Extraordinaire
(1893-1969)

Royal Arden Hickman - a familiar name in any field of design! He was truly a genuis, having a natural affinity for any medium of creativity: paper, crystal, aluminum, silver, clay, wood, etc. A definition of "affinity" would read . . . "the force that causes the atoms of certain elements to combine and stay combined" . . . Mr. Hickman was definitely the "force", combining designs, which "stayed" - and their influence felt for decades. In addition to Mr. Hickman's exceptional abilities, the characteristics seen in his designs were his inimitable trademark!

> NOTE: We are told by Mrs. Ruth Hickman: . . . "Royal Arden Hickman was never address- ed as anything but 'Hick.' He may have in his youth been known as Roy or even Art by some of his young friends, but in his mature years, was only known as 'Hick' and signed many of his sketches and personal drawings with that signature."

Hick was born in Willamette, a small Oregon town, on December 28 1893. His home life was one of strict discipline, his parents being devout Methodists. At age 14, Hick began working for the Willamette Paper Mill, and at 16, was drawing plans for the Mill's new warehouse.

Hick was aware of his artistic abilities. He was a pro- lific artist, having made numerous sketches before age 17. During his 19th year, Royal Hickman left Oregon for San Francisco to attend the Mark Hopkins Art Academy. Upon completion of his study, he left for the Hawaiian Islands to assist in the planning of a large sugar refinery.

Hick's great love for the water and boating made the Islands a paradise. However, this paradise ended for Hick when the United States entered into the first World War. He and his friends were anxious to return home and enlist - but there was no passage money.

Previously, at the post office, Hick had noticed the announcement of a poster contest with a $1,000.00 first place prize. The title would be: "Hawaii in the Summer- time" . . . but who had the money for the paints and brushes? The need was discussed among friends, and money advanced for the necessary supplies. Hick spent three days and nights, locked in his room, working on the poster. As the last bit of paint dried, he rushed his entry to the judge, just ahead of the deadline. To his great pleasure and surprise, he won the first prize. Hick was on the next boat leaving Honolulu for the States.

Hick had worn glasses since age four, having been born with poor vision. This defect kept him from the Armed Forces. Not to be deterred in his desire to help the war effort, Hick took employment in the Todd Shipyards in Tacoma, Washington.

Royal Hickman was a gypsy at heart, always on the move, seeking new avenues of outlet for his creative abilities. During the Depression, Hick established a small construction company and was offered a contract to work on the Madden Dam in the Panama Canal. Not acclimated to the extreme intense heat, Hick suffered a severe sunstroke. The stroke left him partially paralyzed, as well as turning his hair snow-white.

He was taken to California for recouperation and therapy. In order to regain full use of his hands while recovering, he was given clay to mold, and the rest is history! With his pocket knife and a crochet hook, Hick began his long and highly successful association with all manner of artware.

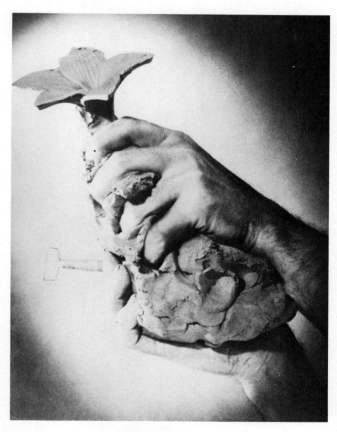

Royal Hickman's creative hands

Hick enjoyed instant success with his vivid colored din- nerware designed for Garden City Pottery, and so, "RaArt Pottery" was born.

> Note: Some of Hick's first pieces were done in stoneware which does not have the brilliant glaze we are accustomed to seeing.

Riding high on previous recognition, Hick was com- pelled to try for the best: the prestigious S & G Gump Company department store of San Francisco. Mr. Gump, although blind, was one of the great art authorities of this time. His decisions were based on the feel of the object. Mr. Gump purchased the entire line, and RaArt Pottery was in full swing. The following photographs on the next two pages are examples of some early RaArt (Hickman) designs.

Figure 8

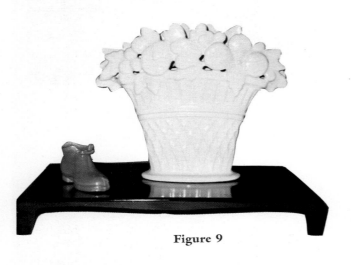

Figure 9

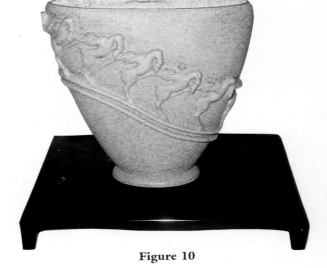

Figure 10

Figure 11

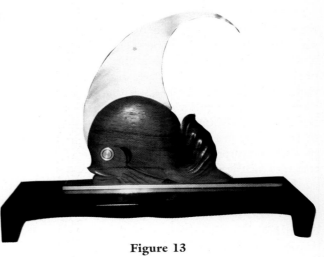

Figure 13

Figure 12

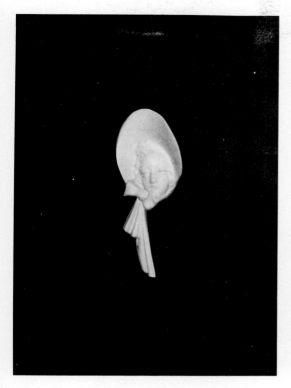

Figure 14

Figure 15

Hick's artistic talent was such that he could not limit himself to just one medium. As he worked with a particular type of material, he would envision the same design in a different substance.

Hick was approached by J.H. Vennon Company of New York for a stint in Europe, designing lines of crystal in Sweden, (for Kosta Glassbruck), Denmark, Czechoslovakia and Italy. Accepting this challenge, he witnessed Nazi domination in Europe, and huge Swastika flags were the "order of the day".

Sadly, most of Hick's designs were destroyed during the occupation, but those surviving were breathtaking in beauty and originality. Hick was intrigued with glass, and upon his return from Europe accepted a post with Kosta Crystal in New York. However, it was not long before he realized that working with crystal lacked the warmth of clay.

The timing was perfect!

Mr. Edmund Haeger, having previously met Royal Hickman through a distributor in California, knew this was the man he wanted to design the new Royal Haeger line. Mr. Hickman was contacted and selected to join Haeger Potteries. In that year of 1938, the "two great Royals" came together, and the Royal Haeger line was launched. It was an instant success!

Mr. Hickman worked closely with the ceramic engineers to help develop the desired glazes. He also did most of his own modeling, although long periods of ex-posure to the clay caused an allergic reaction to his hands. Often the designs were complicated, requiring several pieces to be combined. This procedure was difficult and time consuming, but the results were dynamic. Little extra "stick-ups" were often added for the finishing touch, i.e. flowers, leaves, pieces of wheat, etc.

Hick's black panther, a sleek elongated cat, is prized by Royal Haeger collectors everywhere. The panther was designed for a special (in store) merchandising program for Carson, Pirie, Scott, called "Homemakers". This 1941 design was made in three sizes:

1. 26″ length, tail down, curving upward at the end......R-495

2. 24″ length, tail curled around hind paw.........R-495 (also)

3. 18″ length, tail curled around hind paw.............R-683

This hi-gloss ebony design was a tremendous success!

After the war, the smaller version of the panther was made in "left" and/or "right" positions for use on mantles, as well as various other decor. This 13″ panther carries the R-733 number. The following is an illustration of the mantle grouping, as well the 18″ and 26″ Haeger panther.

— 23 —

A New Haeger Mantle Group

The Gleaming Ebony Panthers with the planter in a choice of Surf Green, Gloss White or Gloss Chartreuse make a striking mantle decoration.

No. 683/3512   Haeger 3 Piece Mantle Set. Set $3.75
Bowl Height 5", Opening 10½" x 3½"
Colors: Panthers Ebony Only—Bowl Surf Green, Gloss White, Gloss Chartreuse

IMPORTANT—*Please refer to Page 54 when placing your order.*
  —*For color description of Haeger Pottery—see page 37.*
  —*PLEASE NOTE: You may now cover all your pottery needs from one shipping point, Macomb, Illinois—see page 1.*
  —*Buy with confidence—we unreservedly guarantee your complete satisfaction with your purchase—see page 54.*

No. 683   Haeger Panther. Each $1.50
Length 18", Height 4½"
Color: Gloss Ebony

No. 495   Haeger Panther
Each $5.00
Length 26", Height 5½"
Color: Gloss Ebony

Arrangements by "Tommy" Bright
Photos by Kistler

Page from *Randall's Catalog,* July, 1950.

At one time, at least 34 other potteries were making panthers trying to duplicate the Haeger panther. Some were produced with rhinestone eyes, gold chain collars and garish trim - but those are not Royal Haeger. The Haeger panthers were marked only with a paper label making identification difficult for the collector if the label had been removed or fallen off years prior. (It is important to keep in mind, that the Haeger panther has no holes for eyes, but a hooded eyelid over the curved mark of the eye).

The 13″ panther also enjoyed success as the basis for TV lamps. The following photo is from the collection of Rudy Corvo. The panther is red, and the shield black and gold. Behind the shield is a tube-style lightbulb.

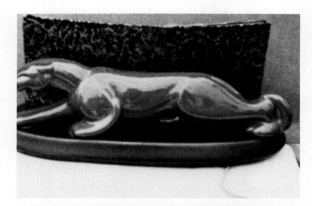

Marshall-Fields was one of Haeger's first customers to use a window display of the new Royal Haeger line. Dudley Crafts Watson, seeing the designs was so impressed he gave lectures regarding this pottery at the Art Institute of Chicago - during the year the line was introduced. Mr. Watson (1885-1972) was a renowned artist, teacher, writer, and lecturer with the Institute.

The public's acceptance of the Royal Haeger artware was instantaneous! The pottery built a second large tunnel kiln to meet the sales demand of their new line.

One year later, in 1939, The Royal Haeger Lamp Company was established. The company thrived, due to its unique and innovative designs. (See page 83)

The operation not only encompassed Hick's designs for ceramic table lamps; it also included his designs for a new line of sterling silver flatware, and one of onyx figures - all from Mexico. Mr. Hickman also designed a group of miniature wood planter tables in four styles: Chippendale, Queen Anne, Duncan Phyfe, and Oriental. To compliment any room decor a line of beautiful, large glass framed pictures, consisting of colorful exotic birds, flora and fauna, was added. As you can see, Royal Hickman's scope of ability in all forms of artistic concepts, was limitless.

> Hick comments: . . . "There's nothing new under the sun. We all use as design media the material which we find at hand in our own everyday life - from birds to animals, from fish to flowers, from a beautiful coiffure to caricatures of hillbillys. And, when once in a while, we really do make something worthwhile, we are complimented by the response."

During Mr. Hickman's tenure with Haeger, as chief designer, his incredible talent resulted in creating highly stylized designs for the Royal Haeger line. The following catalog re-prints represent initial Royal Haeger/Royal Hickman pieces for the years 1938, 1939, and 1940. These early designs are of the utmost importance, having been made BEFORE 1944 (the year in which Mr. Hickman left Haeger's employ).

ROYAL HAEGER

BY ROYAL HICKMAN

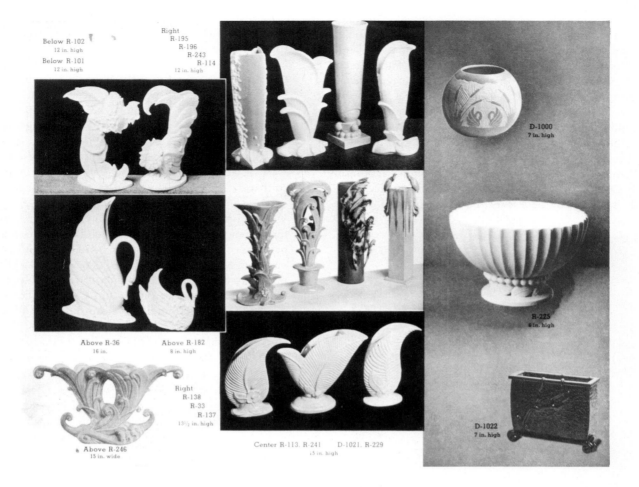

Below R-102
12 in. high

Below R-101
12 in. high

Right
R-195
R-196
R-243
R-114
12 in. high

D-1000
7 in. high

R-225
8 in. high

Above R-36
16 in.

Above R-182
8 in. high

Right
R-138
R-33
R-137
13½ in. high

Above R-246
15 in. wide

Center R-113, R-241   D-1021, R-229
15 in. high

D-1022
7 in. high

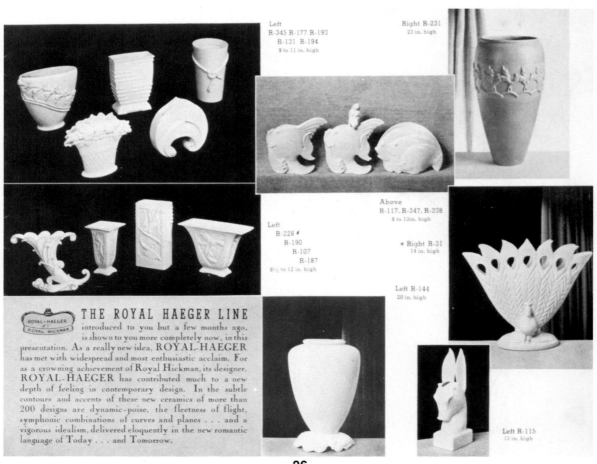

Left
R-345 R-177 R-193
R-131 R-194
9 to 11 in. high

Right R-231
23 in. high

Above
R-117, R-347, R-238
8 to 13in. high

Left
R-228
R-190
R-107
R-187
8½ to 12 in. high

Right R-31
14 in. high

Left R-144
20 in. high

Left R-115
13 in. high

THE ROYAL HAEGER LINE

ROYAL-HAEGER
by
ROYAL HICKMAN

introduced to you but a few months ago, is shown to you more completely now, in this presentation. As a really new idea, ROYAL-HAEGER has met with widespread and most enthusiastic acclaim. For as a crowning achievement of Royal Hickman, its designer, ROYAL-HAEGER has contributed much to a new depth of feeling in contemporary design. In the subtle contours and accents of these new ceramics of more than 200 designs are dynamic-poise, the fleetness of flight, symphonic combinations of curves and planes . . . and a vigorous idealism, delivered eloquently in the new romantic language of Today . . . and Tomorrow.

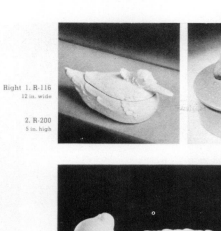

Right 1. R-116
12 in. wide

2. R-200
5 in. high

Right R-209
19 in. wide

Right 1. R-198
11½ in. wide

2. R-188
10 in. high

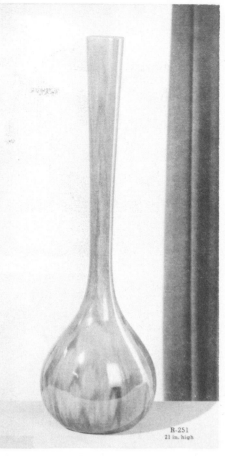

R-251
21 in. high

D-1019
7½ in. high

D-1018
9½ in. wide

D-1020
15 in. high

D-1011
10½ in. high

D-1017
16 in. high

D-1001
7½ in. high

Right D-1004 D-1006
8 in. high 16 in. high

Left D-1023
11 in. high

Below D-1009
7½ in. wide

Below R-184
11 in. high

Below R-235
12½ in. high

ROYAL HICKMAN • DESIGNE

The life and works of Royal Hickman have been suc
urally be of the magnitude of the ROYAL-HAEG
he has explored many fields of creative art, yet has
expression. Today he will tell you that he is never re
of clay "come to life" between his deft fingers.

Right
R-65, R-140, R-140-SB
R-133-3, R-105, R-152
12 to 24 in. wide

Right
R-128   R-20
R-150   R-109
14 to 16 in. wide

Right
Bowl R-112
14 in. wide
Candle Holders
R-185 (pair)
5½ in. wide

Right
Candle Holders
R-173
9 in. wide

Right
Bowl R-133-3B
18 in. wide
Candle Holders
● R-220 (pair)
5 in. wide

R OF ROYAL HAEGER

that his greatest achievement would nat-
ER line. Always a craftsman and creator,
ound no equal to pottery, as a means of
ly happy unless he is busy making a lump

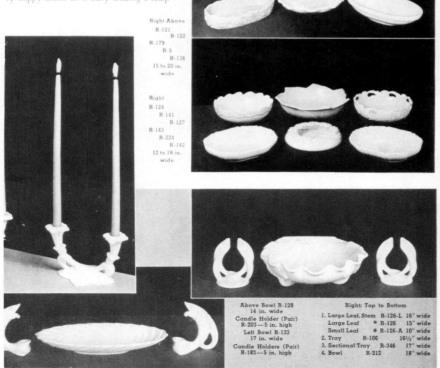

Right Above
R-121
        R-122
R-179
        R-5
        R-136
15 to 20 in.
wide

Right
R-124
        R-141
        R-127
R-143
        R-224
        R-142
12 to 18 in.
wide

Above Bowl R-129
14 in. wide
Candle Holder (Pair)
R-203—5 in. high
Left Bowl R-133
17 in. wide
Candle Holders (Pair)
R-183—5 in. high

Right: Top to Bottom

1. Large Leaf, Stem	R-126-L	16″ wide
Large Leaf	● R-126	15″ wide
Small Leaf	● R-126-A	10″ wide
2. Tray	R-106	16½″ wide
3. Sectional Tray	R-346	17″ wide
4. Bowl	R-212	18″ wide

Left R-161, R-162
9 in. high

Right R-208
16 in. high

Below R-237, R-192
11 in. high

Left
R-218, R-218-B
15 in. high

Below R-180
14 in. high

Below R-168
14 in. high

Left
R-160
R-159
R-158
10 in. high

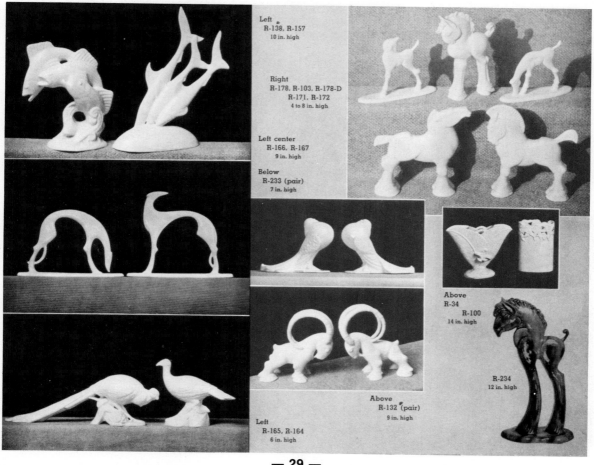

Left
R-138, R-157
10 in. high

Right
R-178, R-103, R-178-D
R-171, R-172
4 to 8 in. high

Left center
R-166, R-167
9 in. high

Below
R-233 (pair)
7 in. high

Above
R-34
R-100
14 in. high

R-234
12 in. high

Above
R-132 (pair)
9 in. high

Left
R-165, R-164
6 in. high

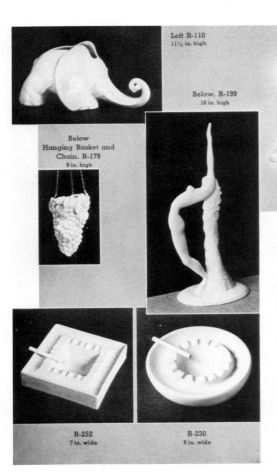

Left R-110
11½ in. high

Below, R-199
18 in. high

Below
Hanging Basket and
Chain, R-179
9 in. high

R-248
10½ in. high

Top R-205   206 (set)
6 and 7 in. high

Bottom R-155, 156, 157 (set)
5½, 6½ and 7½ in. high

R-252
7 in. wide

R-230
8 in. wide

THE HOUSE OF HAEGER

Your own experience with fine pottery will tell you that it is entirely natural that these new, refreshing creations of Royal Hickman should be brought to you by the House of Haeger.

For, with its progress and fame extending through three generations, the Haeger Potteries have nurtured freshness and sincerity in the design and production of decorative ceramics. Creative genius and mechanical skill have worked closely together at Haeger. And together they have made their contributions to the beauty and honest design of fine ceramics. They have created new colors, new textures, new glazes. As you inspect the items in this superb ROYAL-HAEGER line you will see how Haeger skill has supplemented the designs of the renowned Royal Hickman.

R-247
12½ in. high

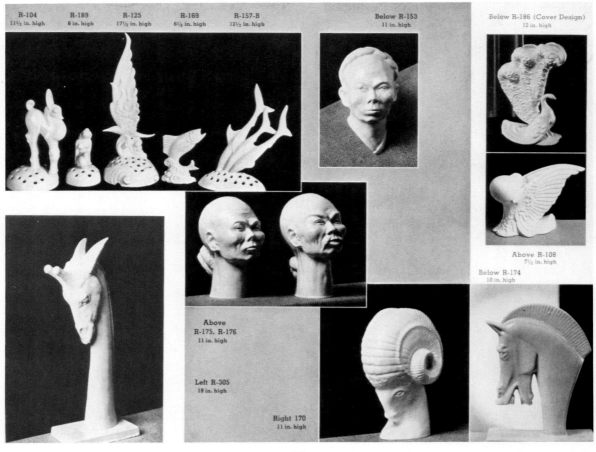

R-104
11½ in. high

R-189
6 in. high

R-125
17½ in. high

R-169
6½ in. high

R-157-B
12½ in. high

Below R-153
11 in. high

Below R-186 (Cover Design)
12 in. high

Above R-108
7½ in. high

Below R-174
10 in. high

Above
R-175, R-176
11 in. high

Left R-305
19 in. high

Right 170
11 in. high

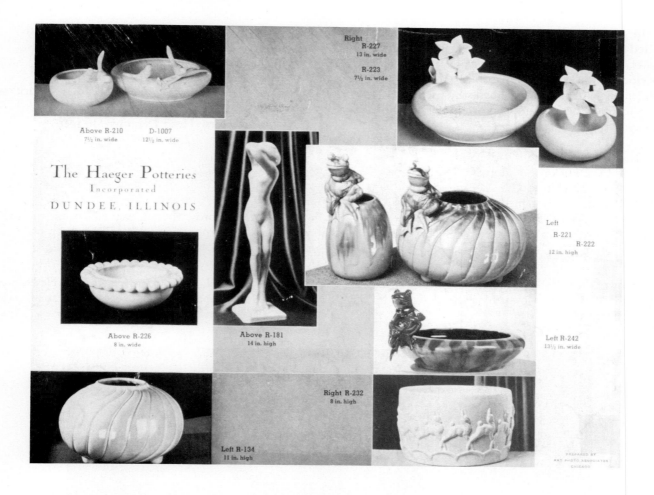

The Haeger Potteries
Incorporated
DUNDEE, ILLINOIS

Right
R-227
13 in. wide

R-223
7½ in. wide

Above R-210   D-1007
7½ in. wide   12½ in. wide

Left
R-221
R-222
12 in. high

Above R-226
8 in. wide

Above R-181
14 in. high

Left R-242
13½ in. wide

Left R-134
11 in. high

Right R-232
8 in. high

"California Designed
by
Royal Hickman"

Figure 16. This label appears on the pair of red swans, 17″ tall, #643, as well as the matching vase, #607, 9″ tall. (Navy blue label with gold trim and lettering)

"Royal Hickman Petty Crystal Glaze"

Figure 17. Pair of Fish Vases, lavendar/blue, 6″ tall R-467 ("Royal Hickman USA-467" incised on bottom).

In pursuing his profession, Mr. Hickman was connected for short periods of time with many different companies, in many different locations (as well as his own operations). It is virtually impossible to track down all the different signatures and trademarks he used.

The following is a sampling of various known markings used, when not designing for Haeger:

1. "Royal Hickman - Paris Ware"
2. "Royal Hickman - Florida"
3. "Royal Hickman U.S.A." (in script)
4. "California Designed by Royal Hickman", label (See figure 16)
5. "Royal Hickman - petty crystal glaze", label (see figure 17)

Many of the very beautiful and rare glass animals produced by The Heisey Company, were designed by Mr. Royal Hickman:

#1550 Fish Bowl (dolphin)	Angelfish Bookends
#1550 Fish Candle	Pouter Pigeon
#1550 fish Match Holder	3 Mallards
Large Swan	Asiatic Pheasant
Cygnet	Wood Duck & ducklings
Gazelle	Clydesdale Horse
Large Horse Head Decanter Stopper	

"In other words, the animals which are the most whimsical in interpretation seem to have been his" . . . these words from Neila Bredehoft.

Clarence Vogel, editor of the Heisey Glass Newscaster, described Hickman as "an artist of exceptional ability, with a very characteristic style".

Royal Hickman designing

BOX 42   DUNDEE   ILLINOIS

"I designed many pieces for Heisey and, of course, I cannot remember all of them . . . the Heisey horses are mine with the exception of the bookends. I think these were in the line before I was associated with them. Giraffe, elephant and mules, etc. are mine . . .

I think the prize pieces I made for Heisey (commercial value) are a pair of penguin decanters in two sizes, the chanticleer cocktail shaker and a cocktail glass with a stem being the leg of a dancer, the leg frosted, or acid etched.

As to the number of animals I made for Heisey I really cannot say, but there were many. In the movie "The Glass Menagerie" they showed all of my Heisey figurines . . ."

(Excerpt from a letter written by Royal Hickman, July 25, 1969)

Royal Hickman, along with Frank Petty and Harvey Hamilton, established a lamp company in Chattanooga, Tennessee. This company operated under the name of Royal Hickman Industries. Subsequently, the lamp company was sold to Phil-Mar Lamp Company in Cleveland, Ohio and renamed Ceramic Arts, Inc.

Hick then traveled on to Florida and started a small pottery in Tampa. Sadly, the pottery was short-lived, being destroyed by fire shortly after production had begun. Returning to Santa Monica, California, Hick designed for Vernon Potteries for a short time, enjoying his return to the West Coast after so many years.

Eventually Hick returned to Guadalajara, Mexico. As previously mentioned, he designed a line of silver for Haeger during the war that was made in Mexico. This author had the privilege of seeing some of the handcrafted solid silver pieces, designed and molded by Mr. Hickman, signed: ''Royal Haeger by Royal Hickman'':

Having accepted an offer from Loza Fina, S.A. Dinnerware in Mexico, Hick built a lovely home in this location (which would become his final resting place). While designing for Loza Fina, Hick also did some of his own artware, but it was far different from any of the Haeger pieces.

Mr. Hickman was once again in the employ of Haeger Potteries in the 1950's, as a free-lance designer and consultant. Hick continued to create his beautiful ''living'' designs until his death in Guadalajara, September 1, 1969.

Eric Olsen

Through the years, many skilled artists have come to Haeger from overseas. These artists serve in various capacities, such as: designers, glazers, and other operators in fields where ''special talent'' is required. The words: ''special talent'' most certainly apply to Mr. Eric Olsen, the renowned Norwegian artist!

Eric Olsen, born Erling Birger Olsen in Drammen, Norway in 1903, began his art training at the age of 11, following through with academic study in Oslo, London, and Paris. While in France, Mr. Olsen started his work in the field of china and porcelain. In the ensuing years, he enjoyed a long association with England's famed Wedgwood and Spode, as well as completing four years of war service.

In 1947, Mr. Olsen accepted the post of chief designer with The Haeger Potteries, Inc. From that time until his retirement in 1972, Mr. Olsen's designs comprised 90% of the Haeger artware and lamp production. Note: Figure 18 portrays Eric Olsen with his first two Royal Haeger lamps in 1947.

Figure 18. . ."My two first Haeger lamps-1947" . . .Eric Olsen.

The Olsen creations are extremely life-like and graceful, exhibiting a certain distinctive flair, not to be duplicated by other designers. Many of these works are on display at the Haeger Museum at Dundee, Illinois.

Certainly one of Mr. Olsen's most popular designs would be the famous red bull. Note: Figure 19 depicts the red bull in all it's glory!

Not only does Mr. Olsen excel in design work, but in sculpting as well. He enjoys wide recognition in art circles for his busts of prominent citizens, among which are: Mahatma Ghandi, Winston Churchill, Carl Sandburg, and Mayor Richard J. Daley. Olsen's bust of the late U.S. Senator Everett McKinley Dirksen was dedicated at the opening of the Chicago Federal Building (now the Dirksen Federal Building) in 1971. His memorial bust of Edmund H. Haeger, son of the founder, was unveiled on the occasion of Haeger's 100th anniversary. This bust is on display at the pottery's Macomb, Illinois plant.

Mr. Olsen merely refers to his portrait sculpting as a "hobby . . . a widely rewarding diversion" . . .

One can only feel pride for this Artist - this genial and gracious gentleman - who not only mastered his skill but made monumental contributions to the artistic history of five different countries.

Mr. Olsen, now retired, lives in the Fox Valley with his family, keeping in touch with the community affairs of Dundee.

Figure 19. This magnificent red bull is the creation of Eric Olsen, produced in 1955. The bull measures 8″ in height and 18″ in length. The bull came in ebony, as well as Haeger red. In 1955, this piece retailed for $10.00. Today, this design is classified as "very scarce." (R-1510)

Finishes, '30s & '40s

From the late '30s, through the '40s and beyond, dramatic and brilliant high gloss glazes were available, as were other treatments and finishes. For example:

The **d'Este** finish (identified by the prefix "D") was a magnesium finish - very stately - but its roughness proved a drawback to the customer and this line was shortlived. The unique d'Este vases were decorated with applied flowers, and my favorite design includes a parrot (macaw) perched on a branch extending from the vase. The designs in this line are few and far between. An example of this finish can be found on Page 4 of the Royal Hickman Catalog dated 1938, 39 & 40.

The **Boko** (also Boco) finish is a very unusual glaze. It is bubbly-like in appearance with an underglaze of pink, green, or white showing through the cracks. Pieces in this finish are also quite scarce.

Design R-270 (pictured at the end of this section) demonstrates the Boko finish. Also, picture #66 in the photo section, depicts R-298 (Cornucopia Shell Vase) done in pink Boko.

Also, by 1940, the Royal Haeger fine art line featured pottery decorated with 24-karat gold - rivaling the gold decorated output of the European potters. Applying the gold required specially trained personnel. (This process is not to be confused with the "Gold Tweed" finish of the '60s).

Examples of various finishes can be seen in the photo section of this Guide.

Another type of finishing work, widely used for the Royal Haeger line is "stick-up." Many of the designs are further enhanced by the addition of small handmade flowers and leaves, deftly fashioned by the talented applique workers. At one time, Haeger employed 14 full-time employees, doing nothing but stick-up. These dextrous handcrafters also assembled other pieces too complicated to be cast in one mold. The applique of separate decorative designs is accomplished by moistening the contact points with liquid slip, and carefully joining the pieces. This unusual technique required a considerable amount of time, as well as highly skilled workers.

A variety of original applique designs and techniques were developed by Arnold Vogel, who, during that period, was head of the casting and finishing department at Haeger. An example of "stick-up" can be seen in the Photo Section (Picture #48), showing R-580 Rose of Sharon Vase, and R-590 Hawaiian Candy Box.

The Studio Haeger line, introduced in the late 40s (Identified by the prefix letter "S") brought with it, distinctly different finishes:

Terre Glaze - "A brand new effect where glaze is so treated as to cause the Red Sand body color to 'glow' through. Terra Glaze is a primitive touch, simple but charming, with the warmth of Provincial to soften the austerity of modern";

Red Sand - Red Sand designates the undecorated casting or body made from native clay. In bisque, the design has an earthy, warm red, compatible with modern interiors; and

Random Texture - An overall raised finish in a stripe-like effect.

Foam Overglaze was new for Haeger in 1951 and Cascade Glaze in 1954.

Although Haeger Gold Tweed Glaze (22K Gold) came into the line a little later, we bring this finish to the attention of the collector as a limited number of pieces are available. These pieces are winter white matte, washed in 22K gold. (See photo section, pictures #14, #15, #16).

While color and finish go hand-in-hand, we wanted to clarify a few of the predominate Haeger finishes used during this era.

R-270—These enchanting tropical fish seem to ride the waves that form this exquisite vase. Illustrated in the new Boko glaze. 15" high.

This represents a very rare Haeger vase, art deco in styling, and silver encrusted. This 1940 design was created for the National Silver Deposit Ware Co. (a New York based manufacturer of silver and gold encrusted wares). As these vases were too expensive to market, only a limited number were made. (Note to the collector: One or two vases in this design style have been seen, minus the silver encrustment). (R-441, 11½″ high)

Royal Haeger Colors, late '30s, '40s, early '50s

The Royal Haeger glazes are so original and unusual that words like "mottled," "drizzel," "foam," "marblized" and "agate" come to one's mind in describing them. The glazes are elegant and definitely eye-catching, captivating the attention of the collector. The magnificent colors and design concept of the Haeger-ware makes it distinct and unique among the collectible pottery market.

The following pages are color charts taken from Haeger's spec sheets, for the years 1941 through the early '50s. As the colors are fully described, these charts will greatly aid the collector in identifying their "treasure."

You will note from these charts that not all glazes were available all of the time, especially during wartime priorities.

Following this section, you will find catalog re-prints (in color) showing a great many of the Haeger glazes used from 1938 through 1950 as well as Royal Haeger designs for the same time period.

1941
Finishes available in Royal Haeger Pottery

Alice Blue - A delicate shade of blue, in high gloss.

Amber - A mottled glossy Amber tone in light and dark shades. A touch of green is added to the base. This is a special finish for the Tiger and Tigress figures.

Blue Agate - A deep Royal Blue in high gloss, blended with a lighter greenish blue tone on the upper part of the piece.

Cloudy Blue - A soft Delft Blue in a cloudy effect. A high gloss finish.

Copenhagen - A rich Copenhagen Blue in a high gloss finish.

Gloss White - A clear white in a high gloss.

Honey-Copenhagen - A glossy Copenhagen blue with a delicate shading of light honey tone on the upper edges.

Peach Agate - A glossy peachtone, delicately interspersed with pale blue.

Mulberry Agate - A deep glossy Mulberry, delicately interspersed with lighter shades of Mulberry and green.

Musty Grey - A very light shade of grey, almost a white, shaded in places with a deeper grey.

Mauve Agate - A blending of delicate shades of mauve, green and blue in a mottled effect.

Gun Metal - A high gloss Gun Metal finish. Used mostly as a finish for bases supporting bowls and vases.

Spring - 1942
Royal Haeger Glazes

1. Alice Blue - A dainty shade of Blue, in high gloss.
2. Mauve Agate - A blending of muted shades of Mauve, Green and Blue in a mottled effect. (This glaze will be supplied until we are unable ot make it due to priorities)
3. Peach Agate - A glossy Peach tone, delicately interspersed with pale Blue. (This glaze will be supplied until we are unable to make it due to priorities)
4. Honey-Copenhagen - A glossy Copenhagen Blue with a delicate shading of light Honey-tone on the upper edges.
5. Mulberry Agate - A deep glossy Mulberry, interfused with lighter shades of Mulberry and Green.
6. Musty Grey - A very light shade of Grey, almost a White, shaded in crevices with a deeper Grey.
7. Cloudy Blue - A soft Delft Blue mingled with White in a cloudy effect. A high gloss finish.
8. Gloss White - A clear White in a high gloss.
9. Blue Agate - Royal Blue in high gloss, blended with a lighter Greenish Blue tone on the upper part of the piece.
10. Mallow - An exquisite blend of Purple, Lavender and Light Blue.
11. Antique Ivory - A rich, Honey-colored shade of Ivory, beautifully marked with a darker shade.
12. Green Agate - A glossy Leaf Green with a Royal Blue and White blending.
13. Amber - Shades of light and dark Amber, strikingly blended.
14. Gun Metal - A Blue-Black metallic finish - restricted to bases of most pieces.
15. French Grey with White - A soft Grey with an undertone of White in a lovely drip effect.
16. French Grey with Mallow - The same beautiful blend with Mallow as the undertone.

1943
Description of figures on the front cover
Mantel Vase with Ornamental Figures
R-282, Vase, Height 8″, Length 10½″, Width 3½″
Available in colors 2, 3, 10 and 13

R-313, Tigress, height 8″, Length 12″
Available in Amber Only

R-314, Tiger, Height 11″, Length 10″
Available in Amber Only

Royal Haeger Glazes

1. Alice Blue - A dainty shade of Blue, in high gloss.
2. Mauve Agate - A blending of muted shades of Mauve, Green and blue in a mottled effect. (This glaze will be supplied until we are unable to make it due to priorities.)
3. Peach Agate - A glossy Peach tone, delicately interspersed with pale Blue. (This glaze will be supplied until we are unable to make it due to priorities.)
4. Honey-Copenhagen - A glossy Copenhagen Blue with a delicate shading of light Honey-tone on the upper edges.
5. Mulberry Agate - A deep glossy Mulberry, interfused with lighter shades of Mulberry and Green.
6. Musty Grey - A very light shade of Grey, almost a White, shaded in crevices with a deeper Grey.
7. Cloudy Blue - A soft Delft Blue mingled with White in a cloudy effect. A high gloss finish.
8. Gloss White - A clear White in a high gloss.
10. Mallow - An exquisite blend of Puple, Lavender and Light Blue.
11. Antique Ivory - A rich, Honey-colored shade of Ivory, beautifully marked with a darker shade.
12. Green Agate - A glossy Leaf Green with a Royal Blue and White blending.
13. Amber - Shades of light and dark Amber, strikingly blended.

Special Notice
Due to government orders now in effect and contemplated, the range of colors available for ceramics is being narrowly restricted. Within the limits of these orders as stated now and as amended, we will do our best to supply as wide and attractive a range of colors as possible. However, it may be necessary to discontinue certain colors without notice; in which case, we will substitute colors as closely as possible on your orders.

1946
Royal Haeger Glazes
Glazes for numbers not shown have been temporarily discontinued.

1. Alice Blue - A dainty shade of blue, in high gloss.
2. Mauve Agate - A blending of muted shades of mauve, green and blue to form a striking mottled efect.
4. Copenhagen Blue - A glossy blue with delicate shading of light honey tones on the upper-edges.
5. Mulberry Agate - A deep, glossy mulberry, fused with lighter shades of mulberry and green.
6. Bone Ash - A light grey with deep shadings in the crevices.
7. Cloudy Blue - A soft, delft blue, mingled with white, to achieve a cloudy effect.
8. Gloss White - A clear white in a high gloss.
10. Mallow - An exquisite blend of puple, lavender and light blue.
12. Green Agate - A glossy, leaf green, with blends of Royal Blue and white.
13. Amber Crystal - Rich shades of light and dark amber, fused with white and delicate green, in a beautiful mottled effect.
14. Gunmetal - A grey-black metallic finish in a high gloss, simulating very closely, actual metal.
17. Red Bronze - An antique copper finish in a high lustre, with the merest suggestion of green shading, denoting age.
18. Ebony - Jet black in a high polish, lending itself well to highlight effects.
19. Terra Cotta - A flat, brownish-orange shade in a smooth-to-the-touch finish.
20. Mauve - Similar to an old rose in a high gloss.
21. Mulberry - A deep, rich, ripened mulberry.
22. Lime - Haeger's famous Victoria green in a gloss finish.
23. Hand-Colored Bisque - Plain bisqueware, hand-decorated in pastel shades.
24. Sand - Desert sand shade in rough, manganese finish.
25. Amber - Light and dark shades, beautifully blended.
26. White Crystal - A striking greyish-green, with an overflow of white.

Permanent Displays

Room 15-100 Merchandise Mart Chicago 54, Illinois	225 Fifth Avenue New York 10, New York	2187 Gordon Rd., S.W. Atlanta, Ga.
712 South Olive Street Los Angeles 14, California	Portland Merchandise Mart 821 N.W. Flanders Street Portland 4, Oregon	102 Terminal Sales Building Seattle 1, Washington

We regret that we will be unable to guarantee delivery this year on orders received after March 1, 1946 as the large backlog of orders will account for our 1946 production, based on the present rate. All orders will be priced in concurrence with existing prices at time of delivery.

NOTE: Dimensions are given in the following order: Width, Height, Length or Depth. All measurements are figured in inches.

New exciting glazes . . . featured during Haeger's 75th anniversary . . . 1946.

Among the many glazes that will be featured during the 75th Anniversary year are:

Greenbriar - A rich mulberry agate highlighted by a white and green spray at the top.

Ciel - A soft mauve with a generous use of honey and blue—a delicate mauve-blue effect, highlighted with honey.

Yellow drip - A Chinese (Ming) yellow body glaze with a honey drip highlighted by soft green.

Lime - A very lush, fresh green with either honey or yellow used as an accent and liner.

Chartreuse - A strikingly modern color, with slightly more yellow than the Lime glaze.

Tomato - A deep rich henna tone, especially well-suited for modern pieces and decor.

Ox-Blood - A deep vibrant red, well-known as a glaze but not available for several years.

Honey Copen - A soft green-blue with a luxurious use of honey as a drip and liner.

Royal Haeger Glazes - 1947

Mauve	White Crystal
Mauve Agate	OxBlood
Honey	Ciel
Copen	Green Briar
Honey Copenhagen	Yellow
Mulberry	Chartreuse
Mulberry Agate	Tomato
Bone Ash	Yellow Drip
Cloudly Blue	Gloss White
Mallow	Green Agate
Amber	Gunmetal
Ebony	Lime

Royal Haeger Exquisite Glazes for 1949

Amber - Amber in light and dark shades, beautifully blended.

Amber Crystal - Rich shades of light and dark amber, fused with white and delicate green in a beautiful mottled effect.

Catseye - The dark green of a cat's eye delicately blended and contrasted with white to provide a brilliant color note.

Chartreuse - A smart modern yellow green planned for use with modern furnishings.

Chartreuse and Honey - A background of delicate chartreuse with an over-glaze of soft honey.

Cloudy Blue - A soft, Delft blue blended with white to achieve a cloudy effect.

Copen - A glossy turquoise blue of unusual delicacy and beauty.

Dark Green - Deep forest green in high gloss.

Ebony - Jet black in high polish, blending itself to highlights.

Gloss White - A clear white in a high gloss.

Green Agate - A glossy, leaf green with blends of royal blue and white.

Green Briar - A warm mohogany richly highlighted with white and green in very high gloss.

Green Crystal - A greyish green with white overflow.

Gunmetal - The smooth polished tone of an old-fashioned pistol, finished in a high gloss.

Haze Blue - A high gloss medium-hued blue expertly blended to give a soft smoky effect.

Honey - The soft clear beauty of honey from the hive.

Honeycopen - Rich blue copen accented with honey tones in a bright high gloss.

Hydrangea Pink - A delicate new pink with a lovely flower freshness.

Mauve - A delicate shade of pink, similar to an old rose, in high gloss.

Mauve Agate - A blending of soft muted shades of mauve, green, and blue to form a striking blended effect in a high gloss.

Mission Marble - A white marbleized effect overlayed in soft brown.

Oxblood - A deep, rich, vibrant red gloss.

Pearl Grey - A rich blend of grey and white suitable for many decorative schemes.

Pebble Black - Grained ebony finish in high gloss.

Pebble Brown - Grained brown finish in high gloss.

Persian Grey - Deep-toned grey for modern color harmony.

Romany Green - Rich green with black overtones to accent design.

Silver Pebble - Grained soft grey in a high gloss.

Silver Spray and Chartreuse - A delicate modern dove grey with a silvery gloss undertone, combined with smart yellow green.

Yellow - A warm, rich yellow gloss.

Yellow Drip - Rich full yellow accented with fresh flowing tones of white and green.

1950
Specifications
Royal Haeger Glazes

Amber - Amber in light and dark shades, beautifully blended.

Amber Crystal - Rich shades of light and dark amber, fused with white and delicate green in a beautiful mottled effect.

Amber Gold - An old ivory with spray of golden dust.

Antique Ivory - A satin finish ivory with honey overtones.

Azure Crackle - Dark green interlaced with Haeger Blue and white with an open net of crackle.

Bottle Green - A deep-toned glossy sage green.

Catseye - The dark green of a cat's eye delicately blended and contrasted with white to provide a brilliant color note.

Chartreuse - A smart modern yellow green popular for use with modern furnishings.

Cloudy Blue - A soft, Delft blue, blended with white to achieve a cloudy effect.

Cygnet Grey - An attractive glossy dove feather grey in high gloss.

Dark Brown - A rich mahogany tone of brown in a very high gloss.

Dark Green - A deep forest green especially suited to today's color treatments.

Desert Red - A rich blend of sunset red and tan.

Ebony - Jet black in a high polish, lending itself to highlights.

Gloss White - A clear white finished in a high gloss.

Green Agate - A glossy, leaf green, with blends of Royal Blue and white.

Green Briar - A warm mahogany richly highlighted with white and green in very high gloss.

Green Crystal - A greyish-green blended with over-tones of white and brown.

Gunmetal - The smooth polished tone of an old-fashioned pistol, finished in a high gloss.

Honey - The soft, clear beauty of honey from the hive.

Honeycopen Blue - Rich, blue copen accented with honey tones in a bright high gloss.

Mauve Agate - A blending of soft muted shades of mauve, green and blue to form a striking blended effect in a high gloss.

Mere Green - A Chinese pastel green in a clear high gloss.

Mission Marble - A white, marbleized effect overlaid on a soft brown.

Mulberry - A rich wine-brown glaze in a high gloss.

Nutan - A deep flesh color in high gloss.

Oxblood - A deep rich vibrant red gloss.

Peachblow - A delicate mottled peach and purple glaze similar to peach blooms.

Pearl Grey - A medium grey blended with white tones to achieve a rich effect suitable for modern decorative treatments.

Plum - Deep Royal Purple planned for today's rich color schemes.

Romany Green - Deep sea-weed green with contrasting overtones.

Silver Spray - Delicate dove grey with a silvery gloss undertone.

Tawny Tan - A light satin maple surface.

Yellow - A warm rich yellow glass.

Yellowdrip - Rich full yellow accented with fresh flowing tones of white and green.

Also, in the early '50s, additional exotic glazes were included in the Royal Haeger line, such as:

Willow green	Green stripe
Surf green	Turquoise green
Green stone	Green boko (boco)
Aqua	Cotton white
White lattice	Tropical briar
Woodland brown	Tortoise brown
Walnut stripe	Mahogany
Fresco blue	Chinese blue drip
Dawn blue	Slate blue
Antique grey	Platinum grey
Charcoal	Dawn grey
Ming rose	Coral
Pebble coral	Pink boko (boco)
Green crystal	

Colors found on the Royal Haeger Ashtrays - Black Wonder crackle, Green Wonder crackle, Mahogany Wonder crackle and Rose Wonder crackle.

Haeger catalog, issued January, 1950.

CANDLEHOLDERS
Mauve Agate

WITH CLUSTERS
Mauve Agate

R-418 DOUBLE CANDLEHOLDER
Green Briar

R-373 BOWL WITH FLORAL DESIGN
Green Briar

Designed and Manufactured by

THE HAEGER POTTERIES, INC.

DUNDEE, ILLINOIS   MACOMB, ILLINOIS

SECTION I
Page 4
Issued Jan. 1950

FEATURE THESE SALES TESTED CONSOLE SETS
FOR ADDED TRAFFIC — FOR EXTRA VOLUME

R-711 CHINESE MUSICIAN
Green Agate

EXQUISITE NEW DESIGNS, SUPERB GLAZES TO PLEASE THE MOST DISCRIMINATING

R-769 LEAF VASE
Green Agate

R-789 TRIANGLE
FISH VASE
Chartreuse & Honey

R-773 SCROLL VASE
Green Agate

R-775 SHIP
Amber Gold

R-790 FIGHTING COCK
Oxblood & White

R-786 MODERN VASE
Green Briar

R-791 FIGHTING COCK
Oxblood & White

R-808 MOUNTAIN LION
Tawny Tan

R-809 GAZELLE
Tawny Tan

Designed and Manufactured by
THE HAEGER POTTERIES, INC.
DUNDEE, ILLINOIS

Page 1
SECTION II
Issued Jan. 1950

SALES TESTED ROYAL HAEGER DESIGNS —
TO PLEASE YOUR MOST EXACTING CUSTOMERS

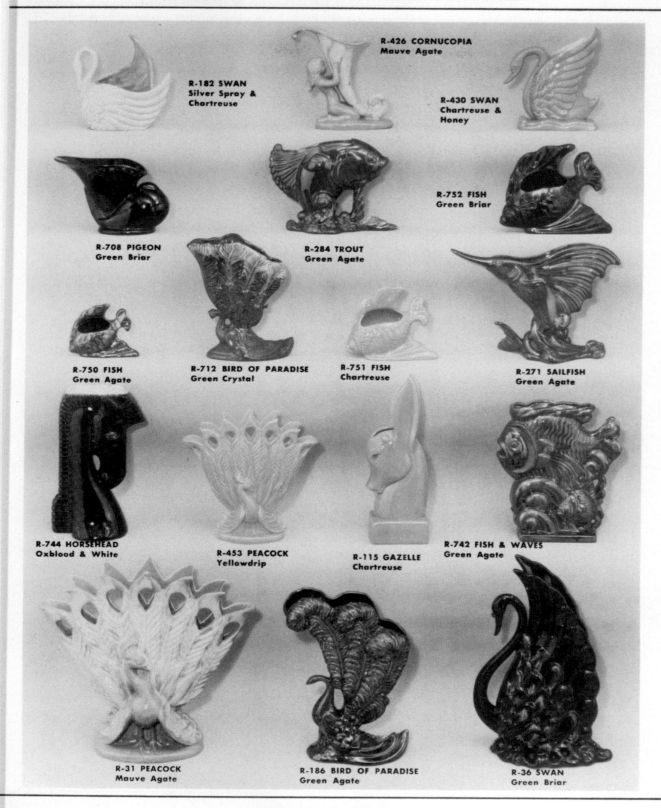

R-182 SWAN
Silver Spray &
Chartreuse

R-426 CORNUCOPIA
Mauve Agate

R-430 SWAN
Chartreuse &
Honey

R-708 PIGEON
Green Briar

R-284 TROUT
Green Agate

R-752 FISH
Green Briar

R-750 FISH
Green Agate

R-712 BIRD OF PARADISE
Green Crystal

R-751 FISH
Chartreuse

R-271 SAILFISH
Green Agate

R-744 HORSEHEAD
Oxblood & White

R-453 PEACOCK
Yellowdrip

R-115 GAZELLE
Chartreuse

R-742 FISH & WAVES
Green Agate

R-31 PEACOCK
Mauve Agate

R-186 BIRD OF PARADISE
Green Agate

R-36 SWAN
Green Briar

Designed and Manufactured by

THE HAEGER POTTERIES, INC.

DUNDEE, ILLINOIS   MACOMB, ILLINOIS

FAST SELLING ROYAL HAEGER DESIGNS
MAKE IDEAL YEAR-ROUND PROMOTION ITEMS

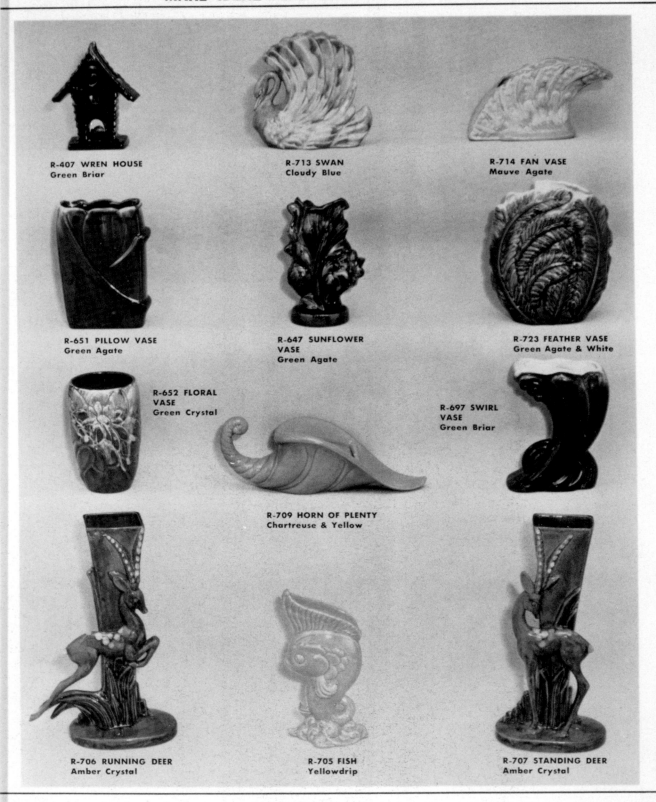

R-407 WREN HOUSE
Green Briar

R-713 SWAN
Cloudy Blue

R-714 FAN VASE
Mauve Agate

R-651 PILLOW VASE
Green Agate

R-647 SUNFLOWER
VASE
Green Agate

R-723 FEATHER VASE
Green Agate & White

R-652 FLORAL
VASE
Green Crystal

R-697 SWIRL
VASE
Green Briar

R-709 HORN OF PLENTY
Chartreuse & Yellow

R-706 RUNNING DEER
Amber Crystal

R-705 FISH
Yellowdrip

R-707 STANDING DEER
Amber Crystal

Designed and Manufactured by

THE HAEGER POTTERIES, INC.

DUNDEE, ILLINOIS

SECTION II
Page 3
Issued Jan. 1950

EXQUISITE ROYAL HAEGER POTTERY VASES
FOR EVERY TYPE AND SIZE FLOWER . . .

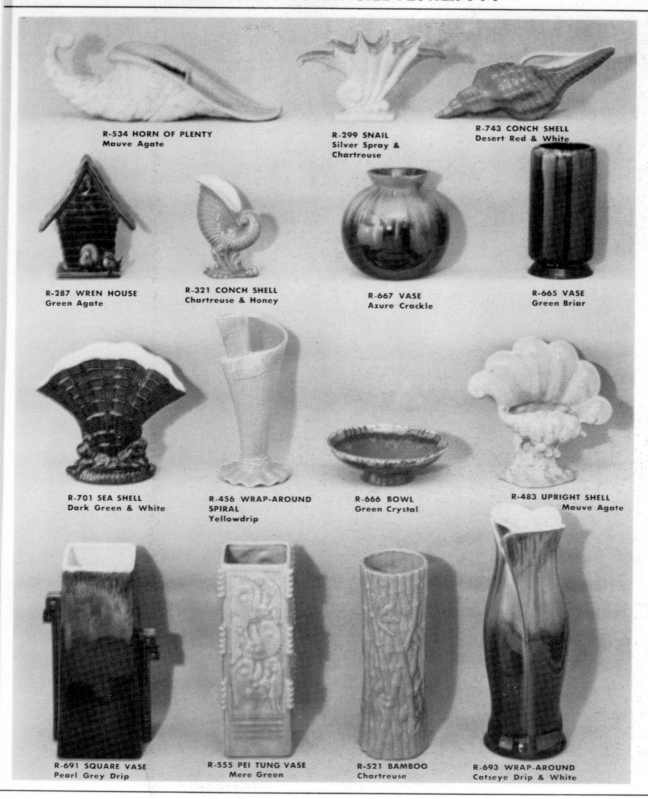

R-534 HORN OF PLENTY
Mauve Agate

R-299 SNAIL
Silver Spray &
Chartreuse

R-743 CONCH SHELL
Desert Red & White

R-287 WREN HOUSE
Green Agate

R-321 CONCH SHELL
Chartreuse & Honey

R-667 VASE
Azure Crackle

R-665 VASE
Green Briar

R-701 SEA SHELL
Dark Green & White

R-456 WRAP-AROUND
SPIRAL
Yellowdrip

R-666 BOWL
Green Crystal

R-483 UPRIGHT SHELL
Mauve Agate

R-691 SQUARE VASE
Pearl Grey Drip

R-555 PEI TUNG VASE
Mere Green

R-521 BAMBOO
Chartreuse

R-693 WRAP-AROUND
Catseye Drip & White

Designed and Manufactured by
THE HAEGER POTTERIES, INC.
DUNDEE, ILLINOIS

Page 4
SECTION II
Issued Jan. 1950

R-716 BUD VASE
Cloudy Blue

R-446 LILY VASE
Silver Spray &
Chartreuse

R-732 LEAF
Green Crystal & White

R-444 LEAF
Green Agate

R-526 PILLOW VASE
Mission Marble

R-496 BUD VASE
Yellow Drip

R-33
DOUBLE LEAF
Green Briar

R-527 PILLOW VASE
Chartreuse & Yellow

R-138
LEAF
Green Briar

R-320 ELM LEAF
Chartreuse & Honey

R-386 BASKET VASE
Mauve Agate

R-301 FAN
Mauve Agate

Designed and Manufactured by

THE HAEGER POTTERIES, INC.

DUNDEE, ILLINOIS   MACOMB, ILLINOIS

BEAUTIFUL ROYAL HAEGER LOW BOWLS
ARE IDEAL FOR TODAY'S FLOWER ARRANGEMENTS

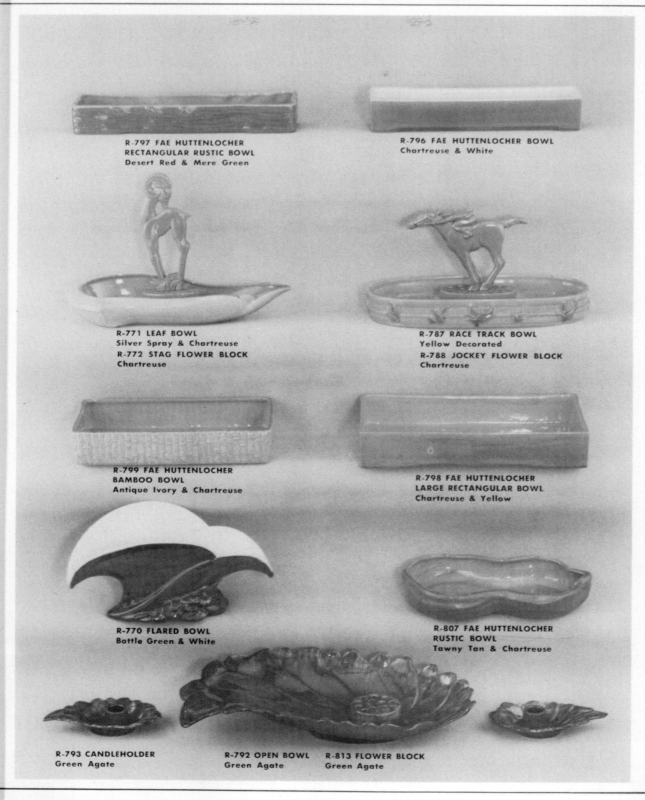

R-797 FAE HUTTENLOCHER
RECTANGULAR RUSTIC BOWL
Desert Red & Mere Green

R-796 FAE HUTTENLOCHER BOWL
Chartreuse & White

R-771 LEAF BOWL
Silver Spray & Chartreuse
R-772 STAG FLOWER BLOCK
Chartreuse

R-787 RACE TRACK BOWL
Yellow Decorated
R-788 JOCKEY FLOWER BLOCK
Chartreuse

R-799 FAE HUTTENLOCHER
BAMBOO BOWL
Antique Ivory & Chartreuse

R-798 FAE HUTTENLOCHER
LARGE RECTANGULAR BOWL
Chartreuse & Yellow

R-770 FLARED BOWL
Bottle Green & White

R-807 FAE HUTTENLOCHER
RUSTIC BOWL
Tawny Tan & Chartreuse

R-793 CANDLEHOLDER
Green Agate

R-792 OPEN BOWL
Green Agate

R-813 FLOWER BLOCK
Green Agate

Designed and Manufactured by
THE HAEGER POTTERIES, INC.
DUNDEE, ILLINOIS

Page 1
SECTION III
Issued Jan. 1950

ROYAL HAEGER FIGURINES FOR EVERY TASTE — FOR EVERY HOME AND GIFT REQUIREMENT

R-721 INDIAN
Desert Red

R-451 MARE & FOAL
Amber Crystal

R-720 MING HORSE
Chartreuse

R-683 PANTHER
Ebony

R-695 LION
Desert Red

R-424 BRONCO
Amber

R-624 TWO DOES
Chartreuse

R-740 GIRAFFE
Desert Red

R-739 HORSE & COLT
Cygnet Grey

R-402 HORSE
Oxblood

R-412 FAWN
Yellow

R-694 BUDDHA
Oxblood

R-103 HORSE
Green Briar

R-413 FAWN
Chartreuse

Designed and Manufactured by

THE HAEGER POTTERIES, INC.

DUNDEE, ILLINOIS   MACOMB, ILLINOIS

SECTION IV
Page 1
Issued Jan. 1950

LOVABLE NEW DOG FIGURINES
THAT SELL ON SIGHT

R-734 COLLIE
Amber Crystal

R-782 SHETLAND PUPS
Amber & White

R-781 MISS PEKE
Amber Gold

R-780 MR. SCOT
Ebony

R-735 COCKER
SPANIEL
Nutan & White

R-736 DACHSHUND
Dark Brown

R-735S SET
COCKER WITH
4 PUPS

R-776 SLEEPING
COCKER PUP
Amber & White

R-777 STANDING
COCKER PUP
Amber & White

R-779 BEGGING
COCKER PUP
Amber & White

R-778 ROLLING
COCKER PUP
Amber & White

Designed and Manufactured by

THE HAEGER POTTERIES, INC.

DUNDEE, ILLINOIS

SECTION IV
Page 2
Issued Jan. 1950

UTILITY AND BEAUTY GO HAND IN HAND
IN THESE PRACTICAL POTTERY DESIGNS

R-718 RAM HEAD BOOKENDS
Oxblood

R-741 BOOKEND PLANTER
Oxblood

R-132 RAM BOOKENDS
Green Briar

R-641 STALLION BOOKEND PLANTERS
Chartreuse

R-638 LEOPARD BOOKEND PLANTER
Amber

R-475 CALLA LILY BOOKENDS
Amber

R-126X LEAF PLATE
Green Agate

R-126A SMALL LEAF
Green Agate

R-286 LEAF PLATE
Green Crystal

R-431 LILY CANDY BOWL
Mauve Agate

R-586 MUG
Green Agate

R-175 FRUIT-FLOWER BASKET
Chartreuse & Honey

Designed and Manufactured by

THE HAEGER POTTERIES, INC.

DUNDEE, ILLINOIS

HAEGER'S WIDE SELECTION OF DISTINCTIVE
POTTERY DESIGNS SATISFY EVERY TASTE

R-754 DONKEY CART
Green Briar

R-540 TURTLE PLANTER
Green Crystal

R-479 PROSPECTOR
Amber Crystal

R-563 ELEPHANT PLANTER
Chartreuse & Honey

R-655 FROG FISH BOWL
Catseye

R-663 SQUARE PLANTER
Chartreuse

R-635 PEI TUNG PLANTER
Yellow

R-657 GONDOLIER PLANTER
Oxblood

R-722 PROSPECTOR
Desert Red

R-656 MERMAID FISH BOWL
Catseye

R-760 LEOPARD PLANTER
Desert Red

R-719 FISH PLANTER
Mauve Agate & White

Designed and Manufactured by

THE HAEGER POTTERIES, INC.

DUNDEE, ILLINOIS   MACOMB, ILLINOIS

SECTION IV
Page 6
Issued Jan. 1950

LOVELY, PRACTICAL DESIGNS IN BON BON DISHES, ASHTRAYS AND CIGARETTE BOXES

R-631 LEOPARD CIGARETTE BOX
Amber

R-632 LEOPARD ASHTRAY
Amber

R-230 COG-WHEEL ASHTRAY
Green Briar

R-669 CUBE CHECKED CIGARETTE BOX
Chartreuse

R-670 CUBE CHECKED ASHTRAY
Chartreuse

R-252 SQUARE ASHTRAY
Green Agate

R-684 TURTLE CIGARETTE BOX
Green Crystal

R-541 TURTLE BON BON
Green Crystal

R-447 SHELL BON BON
Mauve Agate

R-449 LEAF BON BON
Yellow

R-625 ELEPHANT CIGARETTE BOX
Silver Spray & Chartreuse

R-668 SMALL ELEPHANT ASHTRAY
Chartreuse

R-520 BAMBOO ASHTRAY
Chartreuse

R-685 HORSEHEAD CIGARETTE BOX
Oxblood

R-686 HORSEHEAD ASHTRAY
Oxblood

R-567 LEAF BON BON
Green Agate

Designed and Manufactured by

THE HAEGER POTTERIES, INC.

DUNDEE, ILLINOIS   MACOMB, ILLINOIS

Page 7
SECTION IV
Issued Jan. 1950

GENUINE HAEGER POTTERY IS NOW AVAILABLE IN THESE RICH GLOSS COLORS

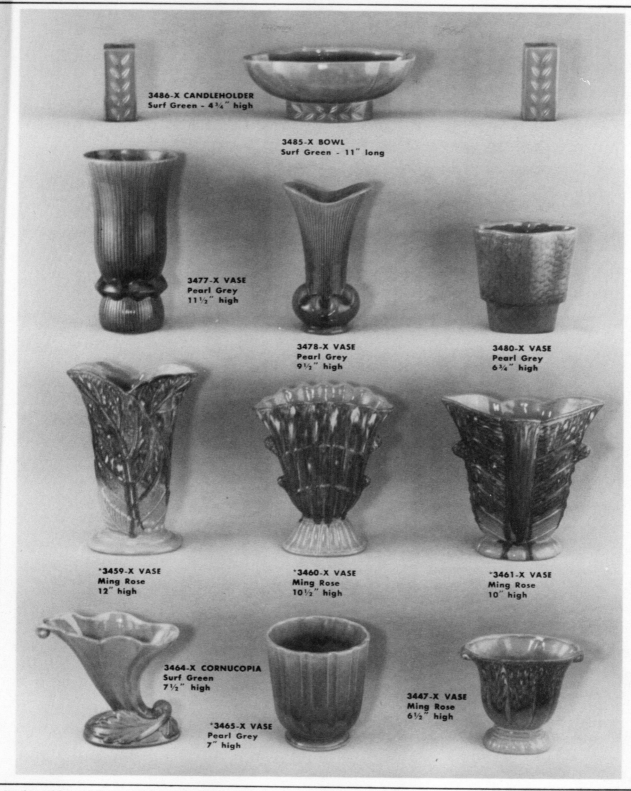

3486-X CANDLEHOLDER
Surf Green - 4¾" high

3485-X BOWL
Surf Green - 11" long

3477-X VASE
Pearl Grey
11½" high

3478-X VASE
Pearl Grey
9½" high

3480-X VASE
Pearl Grey
6¾" high

3459-X VASE
Ming Rose
12" high

3460-X VASE
Ming Rose
10½" high

3461-X VASE
Ming Rose
10" high

3464-X CORNUCOPIA
Surf Green
7½" high

3465-X VASE
Pearl Grey
7" high

3447-X VASE
Ming Rose
6½" high

ce List for Additional Sizes and Color Groups

Designed and Manufactured by

THE HAEGER POTTERIES, INC,
DUNDEE, ILLINOIS   MACOMB, ILLINOIS

SECTION V
Page 1
Issued Jan. 1950

BE SURE TO INCLUDE THESE "Y" DESIGNS IN YOUR GENUINE HAEGER DISPLAY

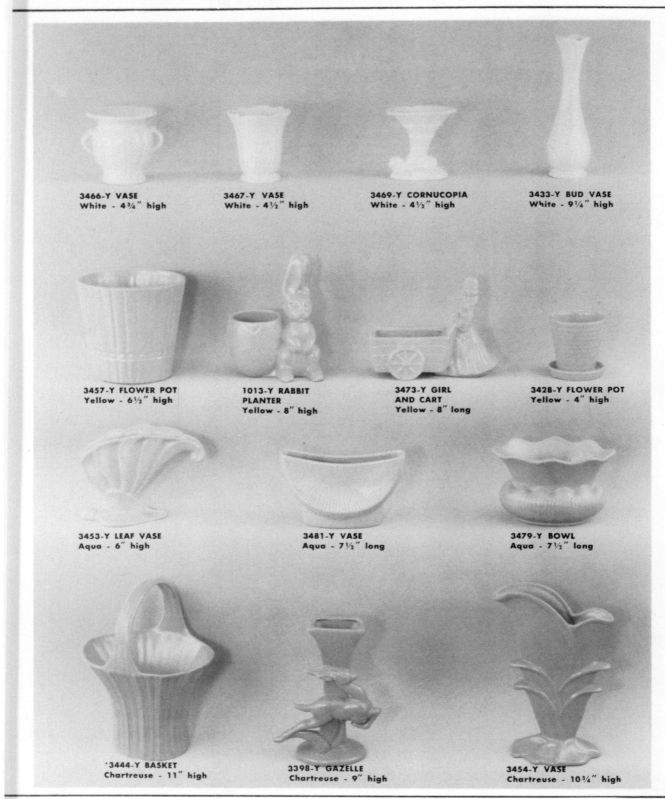

3466-Y VASE
White - 4¾" high

3467-Y VASE
White - 4½" high

3469-Y CORNUCOPIA
White - 4½" high

3433-Y BUD VASE
White - 9¼" high

3457-Y FLOWER POT
Yellow - 6½" high

1013-Y RABBIT PLANTER
Yellow - 8" high

3473-Y GIRL AND CART
Yellow - 8" long

3428-Y FLOWER POT
Yellow - 4" high

3453-Y LEAF VASE
Aqua - 6" high

3481-Y VASE
Aqua - 7½" long

3479-Y BOWL
Aqua - 7½" long

3444-Y BASKET
Chartreuse - 11" high

3398-Y GAZELLE
Chartreuse - 9" high

3454-Y VASE
Chartreuse - 10¾" high

Price List for Additional Sizes and Color Groups

Designed and Manufactured by

THE HAEGER POTTERIES, INC.
DUNDEE, ILLINOIS   MACOMB, ILLINOIS

OUTSTANDING NEW "Z" DESIGNS —
WHITE — YELLOW — WILLOW GREEN — DAWN GREY

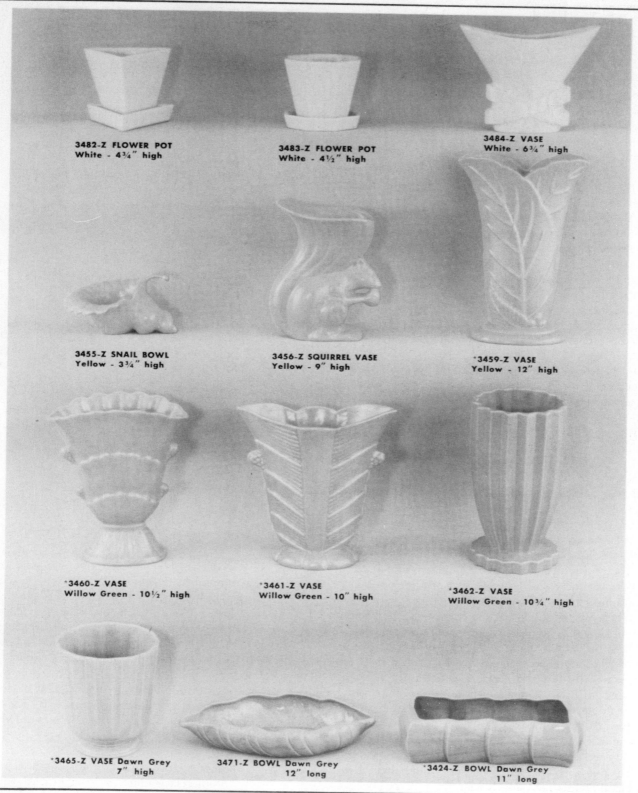

3482-Z FLOWER POT
White - 4¾" high

3483-Z FLOWER POT
White - 4½" high

3484-Z VASE
White - 6¾" high

3455-Z SNAIL BOWL
Yellow - 3¾" high

3456-Z SQUIRREL VASE
Yellow - 9" high

*3459-Z VASE
Yellow - 12" high

*3460-Z VASE
Willow Green - 10½" high

*3461-Z VASE
Willow Green - 10" high

*3462-Z VASE
Willow Green - 10¾" high

*3465-Z VASE Dawn Grey
7" high

3471-Z BOWL Dawn Grey
12" long

*3424-Z BOWL Dawn Grey
11" long

Price List for Additional Sizes and Color Groups

Designed and Manufactured by

THE HAEGER POTTERIES, INC.
DUNDEE, ILLINOIS   MACOMB, ILLINOIS

SECTION V
Page 3
Issued Jan. 1950

Numbering System, 1938 to early '50s

This chapter will deal with the identification and numbering system of the Royal Haeger Line introduced in 1938. As previously stated, Royal Hickman was the number one designer of this line from it's inception until the mid '40s. Therefore, some of the earlier designs will say: "Royal Haeger by Royal Hickman" followed by a number with the prefix "R" (separating it from the regular Haeger line). Other designs will simply say: "Royal Haeger - U.S.A." and a number with the prefix "R". (The signature and numbers are raised). Keep in mind, however, that *not all* pieces designed by Royal Hickman have his name on the bottom. There is no hard and fast rule here.

The Royal Haeger line started with the number R-1, and the pieces were numbered consecutively as they came into the line. Therefore, the *lower* the number, the *older* the design. Also, if the piece is signed "Royal Haeger by Royal Hickman", that would further indicate the 1938-44 time period.

In the late '40s (no definite date can be established), the extra plug on the bottom - necessary for the numbers and signatures - was removed in order to facilitate production. Paper labels were then used.

It is not unusual for pieces made during this transition period to have both a raised number on the bottom, AND a paper label.

We realize, of course, that over the years many of the labels have been washed off, worn off or dried up and fallen off - making identification more difficult. However, as the collector becomes more familiar with Royal Haeger and/or Royal Hickman, the designs have characteristics that are readily identifiable. The designs are unique - soft flowing lines, yet, intricate and strong. Each piece is individual in its portrayal and color. (A totally glazed bottom is also a good indication of Haeger).

When Mr. Hickman left the employ of The Haeger Potteries in 1944, his name was removed from the molds, but "Royal Haeger" with an "R" number remained to identify the line. This explains why you may see the same piece, one with Royal Hickman's name on the bottom, and one without - indiating the design ran before Hickman's departure, and again afterward, with his name removed from the mold.
New molds were made as needed and were retired only when sales decreased.

The following guidelines will clarify and help to identify Royal Haeger pieces of this era. (In addition, be sure to consult the color charts presented in the preceding section).

1. When the original figurine took on a different dimension, i.e. becoming a planter, table lamp, TV lamp, etc. - it also took another number. Examples:

(A) R-809 Gazelle Figurine
R-869 Gazelle Planter
5378 Gazelle Table Lamp
5415 Gazelle TV Planter/Light

(B) R-408 Double Racing Horses Figurine
R-883 Double Racing Horses Planter
5481 Double Racing Horses Table Lamp
5442 Double Racing Horses TV Planter/Lamp

2. When a design came in two sizes, both would have a different number. Examples: R-287 Large Bird House (2 birds) 9½", R-407 Small Bird House (1 bird) 6¾"

3. Haeger's unique mantle sets included designs in the right and left positions , example: 8" swans - R-182R (right-hand position) and R-182L (left-hand position).

4. Collectively, animal sets would have a number, and each individual piece within that set would have a different number.

Example: Cocker with 4 pups. Set, R-7355
Sleeping Cocker pup, R-776
Standing Cocker pup R-777
Rolling Cocker pup, R-778
Begging Cocker pup, R-779

5. Pairs of animals in different positions would have different numbers. Example: Egyptian Cat - head up - R-494, Egyptian Cat - head down - R-493

6. Console sets, usually consisting of three pieces, will have different numbers. Example: Starfish bowl, R-967, matching starfish candleholders, R-968.

Sitting or lying, heads-up or heads-down, small or large, right or left, figurine/planter/lamp - one can safely assume that each design will have a different number.

7. An important contribution in this time frame, was the Studio Haeger line, designed in 1947/48 by Helen Conover, free-lance artist. As the designs originated, they were given a number with an "S" prefix. Later, however, if the piece came into the Royal Haeger line, it was given a new number - with an "R" prefix. (See page 67)

8. The soft matte pieces found with an "RG" prefix number apply to the Royal Garden Flower-ware line. (See page 73)

Over the years, out in the collecting field, the "S" prefix numbers, as well as the "RG" prefix numbers, have become intermingled with the "R" prefix numbers of the Royal Haeger line. Therefore, the preceding items 7 & 8 will clarify the situation.

Collecting Royal Haeger is a great adventure! With or without numbers, and with or without labels, these pieces speak for themselves. Eventually the collector will be able to recognize certain characteristics of the designs created during the '30s and '40s. Some pieces just seem to say: . . . "I'm Haeger - take me home' . . ."

Inquiries accompanied by SASE will be answered by the author.

Labels

The following sketches are representative of the different labels used by The Haeger Potteries over the years.

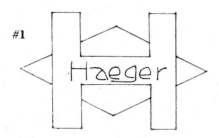

#1

The above sketch represents one of the earliest marks used by Haeger and was probably in effect until the '20s. Also used was a triangle shaped label on the very early pieces.

#1a

Border in Gold
Script & Urn in Gold
Green Background

This label indicates a time period when ALL pottery was made at the Dundee location (before the Macomb plant opened in 1939).

#2

Silver Border
Silver Lettering
Blue Background
Shaded Area Silver

The "Century of Progress" label was used on wares manufactured and sold at the 1934 Chicago World's Fair. (Haeger erected a working pottery on that site).

#3

Gold Border
Green Frame
Gold Background
Green Letters

One type of label used during Haeger's 75th anniversary

#3A

Gold Edge
Green Frame
Gold Background (crown)
Green Letters

Another example of the 75th anniversary label.

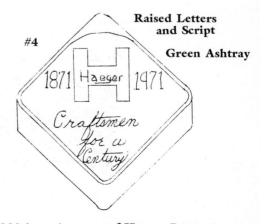

Raised Letters and Script

Green Ashtray

#4

100th anniversary of Haeger Pottery!

#5

Gold Rim - Edge
Background Beige
Hand - Gold
Haeger - Gold
    Background Black
Stripes - Gold

Two more examples of design labels appearing on Haeger's wares.

#6

Silver Background
Black "H"
Silver Letters

#7

Border in Silver
Background Green (Pale)
Letters in Silver

#8

Silver Rim
Green Background
Silver Letters

Regular Haeger line - this green label with silver border and printing, has been seen in other shapes, such as oval, diamond, and rectangular, all appearing on the regular Haeger line.

#9

Gold Background
Black Letters

Haeger label - Macomb plant

#11

Silver Background
Black Letters
Black Edge

#10

White Background with
Green Lettering and Gazebo

1986 Label from Macomb Plant

**NEW ROYAL HAEGER LABEL
FROM DUNDEE PLANT**

#12

#13

Haeger Crowns

**Gold Border & Lettering
Yellow Background**

**Tweed
Gold Border
& Lettering
Black Background**

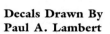

**Decals Drawn By
Paul A. Lambert**

Studio Haeger

New VITAL DESIGNS . . related in design or decoration . . .gifted ceramic artist doing his own designing, modeling and casting, adds with his own skilled hands, the exquisite touches that distinguish his work from "production run" pottery. His output is always limited and the cost of each design limits its sale.

Studio Haeger ceramics parallel the work of the individual gifted ceramic artist, and is a daring new achievement! Purchase of one Studio Haeger design stirs up the desire to complete a full collection.

If there is any one period which seems to characterize Studio Haeger, it would perhaps be "Provincial" in the modern manner.

Studio Haeger is imporant to the collector. Initially, the designs coming into this line were marked with an "S" prefix number. However, at a later time, some of these designs were added to the Royal Haeger line, thus assuming an "R" prefix - with a different number. For example:

Original *Studio Haeger S-229* - prancing horse planter, became *R-1262* when it entered the Royal Haeger line, and #6044, when it became a TV lamp.

(That would account for a design having an "S" number as well as an "R" number). This, however, would be the exception - not the rule - for the Studio Haeger Line.

Studio Haeger Designs

Design Number	Description	Dimension
S-225	Peasant Maid w/2 baskets	15½"H
S-226	Little Sister w/1 basket	11½"H
S-229	Prancing Horse Planter (also R-1262)	10½"H
S-230	Garden Girl (also R-1179)	10½"H
S-231	Lorelei Planter (also R-1257)	15"L
S-232 & S-233	Merbabes (match S-231)	5"H
S-234	Goat Cart	10"L
S-240	Pink Horses Ashtray	13"L
S-241	Sands of Time Ashtray	12"L
S-242	Mermaids Ashtray	12"L
S-243	Ghosts Ashtray	11"L
S-244	CanCan Girl Ashtray	11"L
S-245	Bears Ashtray	11"L
S-246	Tropic Ashtray	11"L
S-247	Raised Jungle Scene Ashtray	13½"L
S-300	Random Texture Table Lamp	23"H
S-300X	(Same as above, with plastic shade)	
S-301	Llama Table Lamp	24"H
S-301X	(Same as above, with plastic shade)	
S-302	Raindrops Table Lamp	24"H
S-302X	(Same as above, with plastic shade)	
S-303	Grooved Cone Table Lamp	30"H
S-303X	(Same as above, with plastic shade)	

S-304	Tempo Column Table Lamp	24"H
S-304X	(Same as above, with plastic shade)	
S-305	Bottle Table Lamp	27½"H
S-305X	(Same as above, with plastic shade)	
S-306	Figure 8 Bottle Lamp	30"H
S-306X	(Same as above, with plastic shade)	
S-400	Random Textured Vase	10"H
S-401	Random Textured Tray	13½"L
S-402	Random Texture Ashtray	6" Dia.
S-421	Llama Vase	10"H
S-422	Llama Ashtray	11½"L
S-423	Llama Figurine	8"H
S-441	Raindrop Vase	10"H
S-442	Tempo Vase	12"H
S-443	Tempo Ashtray	9"L
S-444	Tempo Texture Vase	8½"H
S-445	Tempo Texture Bowl	14" Dia.
S-446	Tempo Texture Candleholders	9"L
S-447	Flat Tempo Texture Vase	7½"L
S-461	Modern Trio Candleholder	9"H
S-462	Tiger Figurine	9"L
S-463	Canasta Box and Ashtray	8"L
S-464	Coaster Ashtray	4" sq.
S-465	Gourd Candleholder	3½"H
S-466	Triple Candleholder	7"H
S-467	Textured Slip Pot	6"H
S-468	Lined Bowl	12"L
S-469	Poi Bowl	11"L
S-470	Poi Candleholders	5"L
S-471	Basket Weave Bowl	6½" sq.
S-473	Large Pitcher	17"H
S-475	Gourd Bowl	9"L
S-476	Fruit Bowl	14½"L
S-477	Oblong Ashtray	11½"L
S-478	Kidney Ashtray	13½"L
S-480	Large Leaf	16"L
S-485	Round Ribbed Ashtray	6" Dia.
S-500	Ridged Bowl	13¾"L
S-501	Ridged Candleholders	4½"L
S-502	Triangle Candlebowl	10½" W
S-504	Triangle Candy Box	8"W
S-507	Window Box	10¼"L
S-508	Double Ashtray	9"L
S-509	Ashtray	8½"L
S-512	Floor Ashtray - Oblong	26½"H
S-515 (also)	Oblong Floor ''Snack'' Ashstand	26½"H
S-515	Round Glass Ashstand	29½"H
S-516	Round Floor ''Snack'' Ashstand	29½"H
S-521	Cog Wheel Ashtray	7¾" dia
S-524	Round Fluted Bowl	10½" dia.
S-525	Fluted Candleholder	4¾" dia.
S-526	Round Swirl Bowl	12½" dia.
S-527	Swirl Candleholders	6" dia.
S-528	Saucer Flower Pot	6½"H
S-533	Gazelle Bowl	10"L
S-533S	Candleholders	6" dia.
S-537	Cone Bowl	13"L
S-538	Laurel Vase	6½"H
S-539	Laurel Vase	8"H

S-540	Laurel Vase	12"H
S-549	Bowl	9" dia
S-550	Bowl	11"L
S-551	"S" Bowl	12"L
S-552	"S" Bowl	11"L
S-553	Window Box	10"L
S-554	Bowl	11"L
S-555	Gazelle Vase	12½"H
S-563	Fluted Window Box	12"L
S-564	Fluted Window Box	15½"L
S-575	Tall Chinese Vase	12½"H
S-576	Window Box	12"L
S-577	2-Level Planter	13½"L
S-578	Figure 8 Planter	11½"L
3669	Duck, head-down	4½"H
3670	Peasant Girl, one basket, "S" shape base	17¼"H
3671	Duck, head-up	7"H
3672	Duckling, head-up	4¼"H
3673	Duckling, head-straight	3¾"H

We cannot attempt to offer pricing on these "special designer" pieces as their output was limited, and therefore scarce in the collecting field. Now and then, a collector will find a Royal Haeger piece with the "S" prefix, and we wanted to clarify its meaning.

The following catalog re-prints will show examples of this unusual Studio Haeger line.

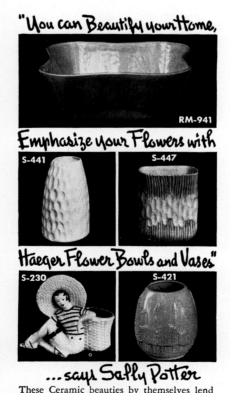

"You can Beautify your Home,

RM-941

Emphasize your Flowers with

S-441   S-447

Haeger Flower Bowls and Vases"

S-230   S-421

...says Sally Potter

These Ceramic beauties by themselves lend color accent and interest to your home; and they're specially designed to make your flower arrangements more dramatic. Remember, for variety of design, glaze and color—for lasting beauty—be sure to ask for Haeger Ceramics.

THE HAEGER POTTERIES, INC.
DUNDEE, ILL.-MACOMB, ILL.
BETTER HOMES & GARDENS, APRIL, 1952

Fall Pottery Catalog 1953

3311—Cat. Ivory, Mint Green, Nut Brown, Charcoal. RETAIL PRICES: $1.70 ea., $18.00 per dz. Height: 7".

3748—CAT & BOWL. Lemon Yellow, Charcoal, White, Nut Brown. RETAIL PRICES: $3.50 ea., $36.00 per dozen. Height: 8".

Genuine & Studio Haeger

THE HAEGER POTTERIES INC., DUNDEE, ILL., MACOMB, ILL., SAN JUAN CAPISTRANO, CALIFORNIA

Studio Haeger Console Sets
Styled for the Discriminating Hostess

TOP ROW

S-500—RIDGED BOWL. White, Green, Sunset Yellow, Chartreuse, Mahogany. RETAIL PRICE: $4.00. Length: 13¾".

S-501—RIDGED CANDLEHOLDERS. White, Green, Sunset Yellow, Chartreuse, Mahogany. RETAIL PRICE: $3.00 pr. Length: 4½".

S-526—ROUND SWIRL BOWL. White, Green, Sunset Yellow, Chartreuse, Mahogany. RETAIL PRICE: $5.00. Diameter: 12½".

S-527—SWIRL CANDLEHOLDERS. White, Green, Sunset Yellow, Chartreuse, Mahogany. RETAIL PRICE: $3.00 pr. Diameter: 6".

BOTTOM ROW

S-533—GAZELLE BOWL. White, Green, Sunset Yellow, Chartreuse, Mahogany. RETAIL PRICE: $3.00. Length: 10".

S-533s—CANDLEHOLDERS. White, Green, Sunset Yellow, Chartreuse, Mahogany. RETAIL PRICE: $3.00 pr. Diameter: 6".

S-524—ROUND FLUTED BOWL. White, Green, Sunset Yellow, Chartreuse, Mahogany. RETAIL PRICE: $3.00. Diameter: 10½".

S-525—FLUTED CANDLEHOLDER. White, Green, Sunset Yellow, Chartreuse, Mahogany. RETAIL PRICE: $2.00 pr. Diameter: 4¼".

Studio Haeger Bowls Designed for Perfect Flower and Fruit Arrangement

TOP ROW

S-502—TRIANGLE CANDLEBOWL.
White, Green, Sunset Yellow,
Chartreuse, Mahogany. RETAIL
PRICE: $3.50. Width: 10½".

S-480—LARGE LEAF BOWL.
White, Green, Sunset Yellow,
Chartreuse, Mahogany. RETAIL
PRICE: $6.00. Length: 16".

S-472—SALAD BOWL. White,
Green, Sunset Yellow, Chartreuse,
Mahogany. RETAIL PRICE: $3.50.
Diameter: 11¼".

MIDDLE ROW

S-549—BOWL. White, Green,
Sunset Yellow, Chartreuse, Ma-
hogany. RETAIL PRICE: $2.50.
Length: 9".

S-537—CONE BOWL. White,
Green, Sunset Yellow, Chartreuse,
Mahogany. RETAIL PRICE: $3.50.
Length: 13".

S-550—BOWL. White, Green,
Sunset Yellow, Chartreuse, Ma-
hogany. RETAIL PRICE: $3.00.
Length: 11".

BOTTOM ROW

S-554—BOWL. White, Green,
Sunset Yellow, Chartreuse, Ma-
hogany. RETAIL PRICE: $2.00.
Length: 10½".

S-551—"S" BOWL. White, Green,
Sunset Yellow, Chartreuse, Ma-
hogany. RETAIL PRICE: $2.50.
Length: 12".

S-552—"S" BOWL. White, Green,
Sunset Yellow, Chartreuse, Ma-
hogany. RETAIL PRICE: $3.50.
Length: 14".

Important Vases and Figurines for Every Taste

TOP ROW

S-555—GAZELLE VASE. White, Green, Sunset Yellow, Chartreuse,
Mahogany. RETAIL PRICE: $3.00. Height: 12½".
S-400—RANDOM TEXTURED VASE. White, Green, Sunset Yellow,
Chartreuse, Mahogany. RETAIL PRICE: $4.00. Height: 10".
S-575—TALL CHINESE VASE. White, Green, Sunset Yellow, Char-
treuse, Mahogany. RETAIL PRICE: $3.00. Height: 12½".

BOTTOM ROW

S-540—LAUREL VASE. White, Green, Sunset Yellow, Chartreuse,
Mahogany. RETAIL PRICE: $4.00 ea. Height: 12".
S-539—LAUREL VASE. White, Green, Sunset Yellow, Chartreuse,
Mahogany. RETAIL PRICE: $3.50 ea. Height: 8".
S-538—LAUREL VASE. White, Green, Sunset Yellow, Chartreuse,
Mahogany. RETAIL PRICE: $2.50 ea. Height: 6½".
S-473—LARGE PITCHER. White, Green, Sunset Yellow, Chartreuse,
Mahogany. RETAIL PRICE: $6.00. Height: 17".

3670—PEASANT GIRL. Gloss White/Fern Green, Gloss White/Mint
Green. RETAIL PRICE: $10.00 ea. Height: 17½".
3669—DUCK. White/Decorated. RETAIL PRICE: $2.00. Height:
4½".
3671—DUCK. White/Decorated. RETAIL PRICE: $2.00. Height: 7".

3672—DUCKLING. Transparent Yellow. RETAIL PRICES: 60c ea.,
$6.00 per doz. Height: 4¼".
3673—DUCKLING. Transparent Yellow. RETAIL PRICES: 60c ea.,
$6.00 per doz. Height: 3¼".

S-553—WINDOW BOX. White, Green, Sunset Yellow, Chartreuse, Mahogany. RETAIL PRICE: $3.00 ea. Length: 10".

S-578—FIGURE "8" PLANTER. White, Green, Sunset Yellow, Chartreuse, Mahogany. RETAIL PRICE: $5.00 ea. Length: 11½".

S-577—TWO LEVEL PLANTER. White, Green, Sunset Yellow, Chartreuse, Mahogany. RETAIL PRICE: $3.50 ea. Length: 13½".

MIDDLE ROW

S-564—FLUTED WINDOW BOX. White, Green, Sunset Yellow, Chartreuse, Mahogany. RETAIL PRICE: $3.50 ea. Length: 15½".

S-528—SAUCER FLOWER POT. White, Green, Sunset Yellow, Chartreuse, Mahogany. RETAIL PRICE: $3.50 ea. Height: 6½".

S-563—FLUTED WINDOW BOX. White, Green, Sunset Yellow, Chartreuse, Mahogany. RETAIL PRICE: $2.50 ea. Length: 12".

BOTTOM ROW

S-507—WINDOW BOX. White, Green, Sunset Yellow, Chartreuse, Mahogany. RETAIL PRICE: $2.50 ea. Length: 10½".

S-576—WINDOW BOX. White, Green, Sunset Yellow, Chartreuse, Mahogany. RETAIL PRICE: $2.50 ea. Length: 12".

Designed Especially for Window Box Gardeners!

Proved Studio Haeger Smoking Accessories That Mean Extra Turnover

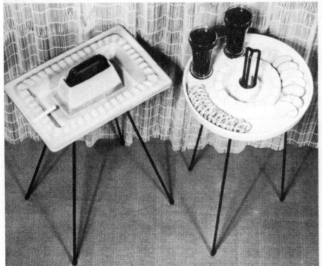

LEFT TO RIGHT, TOP ROW

S-508—DOUBLE ASHTRAY. White, Green, Sunset Yellow, Chartreuse, Mahogany. RETAIL PRICE: $2.50 ea. Length: 9".

S-504—TRIANGLE CANDY BOX. White, Green, Sunset Yellow, Chartreuse, Mahogany. RETAIL PRICE: $3.00 ea. Width: 8".

S-509—ASHTRAY. White, Green, Sunset Yellow, Chartreuse, Mahogany. RETAIL PRICE: $2.50 ea. Length: 8½".

BOTTOM ROW

S-485—ROUND RIBBED ASHTRAY. White, Green, Sunset Yellow, Chartreuse, Mahogany. RETAIL PRICE: $2.00 ea. Diameter: 6".

S-521—COG WHEEL ASHTRAY. White, Green, Sunset Yellow, Chartreuse, Mahogany. RETAIL PRICE: $3.00 ea. Diameter: 7¾".

S-512—FLOOR ASHTRAY. White, Green, Sunset Yellow, Chartreuse, Mahogany. RETAIL PRICE: $10.00. Height: 26½".

S-515—ROUND GLASS ASH STAND. White, Green, Sunset Yellow, Chartreuse, Mahogany. RETAIL PRICE: $10.00. Height: 29½".

The **Haeger** *Potteries* INC.

MACOMB, ILL., SAN JUAN CAPISTRANO, CALIF.

All Prices Subject to Customary Discount

Printed in U.S.A.

Haeger Flower-ware

Haeger's Royal Garden Flower-ware line was design-ed by Elsa Ken Haeger, (sister of Edmund H. Haeger). This new style of body called "porceramic" has a strong structure but isn't thick and heavy like old-fashioned pot-tery. It has a smooth resonant hardness that "rings like rare old porcelain".

The Royal Garden Flower-ware line, established in 1954, was in production for nine years . . . its last design number being in 1963. The Royal Garden line was numbered consecutively, beginning with Design #1, and using the "RG" prefix. The final design number for this line is RG-198. (Once again, the lower the number, the older the piece).

This lovely and graceful Flower-ware line included such items as vases, jardinieres, planters, low bowls, candlesticks, and pitchers, as well as a selection of figurines, adaptable to any arrangement. The classic styling of this line com-plimented but never competed with its floral offerings.

The soft matte finishes were reminiscent of the early '30s, with the '50s treatment. The muted glazes of cinna brown, moonstone white, dawn rose, patina green, matte black, soft yellow, sandalwood, charcoal, and geranium green, were in definite contrast to the brilliant hues of the Royal Haeger line.

General pricing for this Royal Garden Flower-ware line seems to indicate categories of small, medium, and large pieces being priced from $3.00, $5.00 and $8.00 (respec-tively). At this point, there is not enough Royal Garden being found to establish definite values.

Listed below are samples of the "RG" line:

RG- 1 16″ window box
2 12″ window box
3 14″ round bowl
4 12″ rectangular bowl
5 9″ rectangular bowl
6 6″ rectangular bowl
7 10″ square bowl
8 8″ square bowl
9 6″ square bowl
10 9″ square planter
11 10″ round planter
12 12″ rectangular planter bowl
13 12″ pillow vase
14 9″ pillow vase
15 6″ pillow vase
16 9″ bud vase
17 11½″ tall madonna planter
18 9″ madonna planter
19 9″ round Grecian Urn
20 8½″ oval Grecian Urn
21 8″ hospital vase
22 11″ vase
23 12″ vase
24 14″ bell shaped vase

RG-25 13″ gladiola vase
26 10″ gladiola vase
27 5½″ rose bowl
28 6″ rose bowl
29 6″ wrap-around rose bowl
30 4″ flower pot
31 6″ flower pot
32 8″ flower pot
33 3¼″ candleholder
34 4¾″ standing swan figurine
35 4½″ feeding swan figurine
36 9″ triangular bowl
37 6″ triangular bowl
38 6″ pouter pigeon
39 3½″ flower pitcher
40 4½″ small posy bowl
41 14½″ large pitcher
42 10″ medium flower pitcher
43 12″ strawberry jar
44 21″ long-log planter
45 17″ long-fluted box planter
46 25″ bird bath
47 12″ garden urn
48 9″ round bowl

. . . Rings Like Rare Old Porcelain. .

The following pages are catalog re-prints from the Haeger files. Also, photo #13 (in the photo section) is an example of shapes and colors for this line.

Figure 20 defines additional Royal Garden shapes and is courtesy of Mrs. Betty Latty Hurlburt).

1954 Haeger Flower-ware catalog

Haeger® OFFERS YOU A BRAND NEW HEAVY TRAFFIC DEPARTMENT WITH THIS NEW DISPLAY RACK

Yours for $15.00 with a $50.00 order.
Yours for $10.00 with a $100.00 order.

Limit of two to a customer.
Please indicate how many desired.

RG 19—ROUND GRECIAN URN.
Height: 9". Retail Price $5.00.

RG 10—9" SQUARE PLANTER
BOWL. Retail Price $2.00.

RG 20—OVAL GRECIAN URN.
Height: 8½". Retail Price $3.00.

RG 16—9" BUD VASE.
Retail Price $1.20.

RG 36—TRIANGULAR BOWL.
Width: 9". Retail Price $1.50.

RG 21—8" HOSPITAL VASE.
Retail Price $1.20.

(All available in Moonstone White, Dawn Rose, Sandalwood, Charcoal, and Geranium Green)

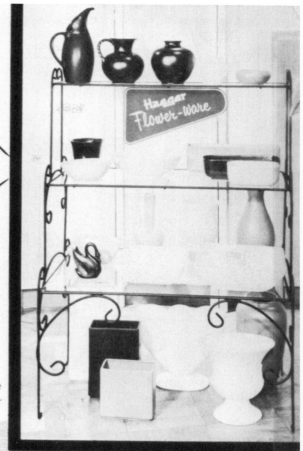

Haeger Flower-ware
Display Rack.

THE HAEGER POTTERIES INC. • 7 MAIDEN LANE • DUNDEE, ILLINOIS

Planters, vases and urns for all occasions

RG 41—LARGE PITCHER.
Height: 14½". Retail Price $3.00.

(All available in Moonstone White, Dawn Rose, Sandalwood, Charcoal, and Geranium Green)

**RG 11—10" ROUND PLANTER
BOWL.** Retail Price $2.50.

**RG 42—MEDIUM FLOWER
PITCHER.** Height: 10".
Retail Price $2.00.

RG 2—12" WINDOW BOX.
Retail Price $2.00.

**RG 12—12" RECTANGULAR
PLANTER BOWL.**
Retail Price $2.50.

RG 1—16" WINDOW BOX.
Retail Price $3.00.

A selection of Flowerware Figurines will compliment every arrangement.

ROYAL HAEGER
Flower-ware
IS STYLED TO EXACTING FLOWER ARRANGEMENT SPECIFICATIONS

RG 28—6" ROSE BOWL.
Retail Price $1.50.

(All available in Moonstone White, Dawn Rose, Sandalwood, Charcoal, and Geranium Green)

RG 13—12" PILLOW VASE.
Retail Price $3.00.

RG 14—9" PILLOW VASE.
Retail Price $2.00.

RG 15—6" PILLOW VASE.
Retail Price $1.50.

RG 29—WRAP AROUND
ROSE BOWL. Height: 6".
Retail Price $2.00.

RG 28—6" ROSE BOWL.
Retail Price $1.50.

RG 27—5½" ROSE BOWL.
Retail Price $1.50.

THE HAEGER POTTERIES INC. • 7 MAIDEN LANE • DUNDEE, ILLINOIS

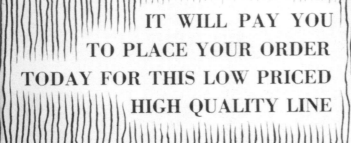

IT WILL PAY YOU
TO PLACE YOUR ORDER
TODAY FOR THIS LOW PRICED
HIGH QUALITY LINE

RG 5—9" RECTANGULAR
BOWL. Retail Price $1.50.

RG 4—12" RECTANGULAR
BOWL. Retail Price $2.00.

RG 5—9" RECTANGULAR
BOWL. Retail Price $1.50.

RG 6—6" RECTANGULAR
BOWL. Retail Price $1.00.

RG 7—10" SQUARE BOWL.
Retail Price $2.50.

RG 8—8" SQUARE BOWL.
Retail Price $1.50.

RG 9—6" SQUARE BOWL.
Retail Price $1.00.

*(All available in Moonstone White, Dawn Rose,
Sandalwood, Charcoal, and Geranium Green)*

Flower-ware ®

RG 30—4" FLOWER POT.
Retail Price $1.20.

RG 31—6" FLOWER POT.
Retail Price $1.50

RG 32—8" FLOWER POT.
Retail Price $2.50.

RG 17—TALL MADONNA
PLANTER. Height: 11¼".
Retail Price $2.00.

RG 18—MADONNA PLANTER.
Height: 9". Retail Price $2.00.

*(Available in Moonstone White,
Dawn Rose, Sandalwood)*

RG 39—FLOWER PITCHER.
Height: 3½". Retail Price $1.00.

RG 28—6" ROSE BOWL.
Retail Price $1.50.

RG 40—SMALL POSY BOWL.
Width: 4½". Retail Price $.80.

RG 37—6" TRIANGULAR BOWL.
Retail Price $1.00.

RG 35—FEEDING SWAN
FIGURINE. Height: 4½".
Retail Price $.80.

RG 34—STANDING SWAN
FIGURINE. Height: 4¾".
Retail Price $.80.

*(All available in Moonstone
White, Dawn Rose, Sandalwood,
Charcoal, Geranium Green)*

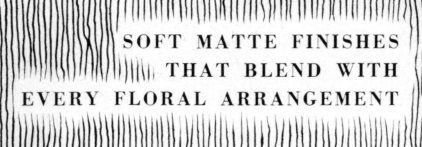

SOFT MATTE FINISHES
THAT BLEND WITH
EVERY FLORAL ARRANGEMENT

RG 7—10" SQUARE BOWL.
Retail Price $2.50.

RG 33—SINGLE CANDLE-
HOLDER. 3¼" Square.
Retail Price $1.50 pr.

RG 7—10" SQUARE BOWL.
Retail Price $2.50.

RG 35—FEEDING SWAN
FIGURINE. Height: 4½".
Retail Price $.80.

RG 5—9" RECTANGULAR BOWL.
Retail Price $1.50.

RG 34—STANDING SWAN
FIGURINE. Height: 4¾".
Retail Price $.80.

RG 38—POUTER PIDGEON.
Height: 6". Retail Price $1.50.

RG 3—14" ROUND BOWL.
Retail Price $4.00.

*(All available in Moonstone
White, Dawn Rose, Sandalwood,
Charcoal, Geranium Green)*

THE HAEGER POTTERIES INC. • 7 MAIDEN LANE • DUNDEE, ILLINOIS

OUTSTANDING VASE VALUES IN ROYAL HAEGER

Flower-ware

RG 25—13" GLAD VASE.
Retail Price $5.00.

RG 26—10" GLAD VASE.
Retail Price $4.00.

RG 23—12" VASE.
Retail Price $3.00.

RG 22—11" VASE.
Retail Price $1.50.

RG 24—BELL SHAPED VASE.
Height: 14". Retail Price $4.00.

(All available in Moonstone White, Dawn Rose, Sandalwood, Charcoal, and Geranium Green)

THE HAEGER POTTERIES INC. • 7 MAIDEN LANE • DUNDEE, ILLINOIS

Figure 20

"Custom-Built" Planters and Window Boxes

Haeger Pottery is a full-profit line the year 'round

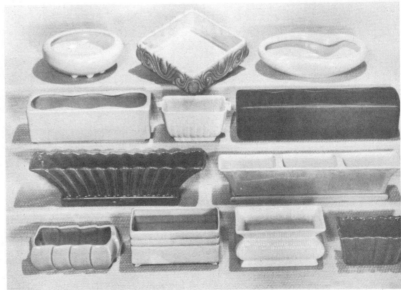

MACOMB, ILL., SAN JUAN CAPISTRANO, CALIFORNIA

Lovely Haeger Madonnas

Royal Haeger Lamps

In 1939, the Royal Haeger Lamp Company was formed. Combining the expertise and versatility of Edmund H. Haeger, Joseph F. Estes and Royal A. Hickman could only bring success - and it did!

Royal Haeger lamps quickly took their place of prominence along with Haeger's existing line of pottery. There was nothing quite like them on the market! (The lamps, of course, were smaller than today's styling). Their totally different design concept and arresting beauty made a Haeger lamp the sign of discriminating taste.

Many of the initial Royal Haeger figurine designs were used as a basis for the lamp styling, carrying through with decorated shades and matching finials. It is interesting to note the various ways in which Mr. Hickman gave continuity to his lamps, creating an over-all coordinated look. For example: the base of lamp Model #4081 (shown in this section) consists of jockeys atop racing horses. Then, Hick would go to Arlington race track, pick up the tote tickets, and paste them on the shade - thus creating a unique blending of the pieces. Adding the matching finial, was like the "icing on the cake".

By 1940, scarcely one year later, the Royal Haeger Lamp Company was an overwhelming success! The following is an excerpt from a newspaper article dated July 9, 1940:

"An exhibition by the Royal Haeger Lamp Company of Dundee, at the Chicago Lamp Show recently closed, has been one of the sensations of that important trade event and has resulted in an unprecedented popularity and business increase for the local items. Joseph Estes, head of the Lamp Company, has been in charge of the Chicago exhibition, and will be in charge of another showing two weeks from now at the gift show at the Merchandise Mart where the lamp show has been staged. Next week, Royal Hickman will go to New York to have charge of the Company's exhibit at the show there . . ."

The following pages depict early Royal Haeger lamps, designed by Royal Hickman. Recognizing these vintage designs is of paramount importance to the collector. Sadly, in most instances, the Royal Haeger lamps were marked with a sticker only. (Occasionally, an "R" number will appear on a lamp).

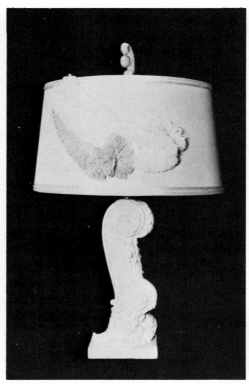

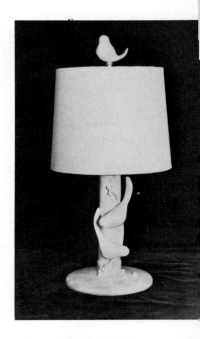

During the war, there was a shortage of electrical supplies, and though the demand for Haeger lamps continued, the orders could not always be filled due to this shortage. It was during this time that Mr. Hickman left the employ of Haeger and started his own lamp company in Chattanooga, Tennessee.

Eric Olsen filled the post of chief designer for the pottery in 1947, filling the gap left by Royal Hickman. The ensuing 25 years were filled with Mr. Olsen's beautiful contemporary ceramic designs.

All Royal Haeger lamps were produced at the Dundee, Illinois location from 1939 until 1969. At that point in time, the Western Stoneware plant in Macomb, Illinois, was purchased. Undergoing renovation and modernization, this plant became the "new home" of the Royal Haeger Lamp Company.

Part of the Macomb plant was converted to mold storage and continuous mold casting. A large plate conveyor was installed, enabling plaster molds to be poured on the moving conveyor. In addition, a finishing line conveyor was built, which would receive ware from all the production lines. A system of storing blocks and cases for the entire company is located there.

Slip is received by truck and stored in an agitated tank under the floor, then pumped to an overhead tank as needed for casting.

After casting and room drying, the lamp bases are spray glazed. Drying of the cast pieces is done in a hanging position, since they are so large. (See Figure 21)

In 1979, Nicholas Haeger Estes was appointed President of The Royal Haeger Lamp Company:

"From the designer who first sees a vision of line and form . . . . to the chemists and engineers who are the link between imagination and creation . . . to the ceramists who use the finest materials and greatest care to creating an idea in three dimensions, our family and staff is proud to put on each finished piece, the name that stands for over a century of quality - Haeger . . ."

Designs are constantly changing, and usually at Haeger, new and major introducitons to the line are made twice a year (January and July). Decal application, hand-decorating, glaze spraying, and the hand application of 22 karat gold, are some of the processess used on Royal Haeger lamp bases.

Today, as in the past, beautiful Royal Haeger lamps can be purchased in stores selling quality products.

Figure 21. Lamp bases hanging from conveyor belt for air drying.

No original catalogs were available for the Royal Haeger lamps of the '30s & '40s. Therefore, we have given the design number, height, and description - taken from Haeger's inventory records. This applies to the TV lamps as well.

All lamps were marked with labels only. If the label is gone, identification may be difficult until the collector becomes familiar with the Haeger glazes and styles. The "Haeger look" includes matching finials, as well as decorator lampshades. Each shade was custom designed to enhance the overall lamp design statement.

Only the figurine lamps will be itemized here, with descriptions to help verify the piece. Additional informa-tion and pictures can be seen in the photo section of this Guide.

(Where possible, we have included the original "R" number, when the same figurine has been used for the lamp base).

General pricing for the Royal Haeger Lamps would in-dicate: $40.00-45.00 price range for the figurine table lamps; $25.00-30.00 for the non-figurine table lamps; and $20.00-25.00 for TV lamps (complete). We have found these prices to prevail, wherever we found *identifiable* Royal Haeger Lamps. Scarcity of design will demand a higher price.

The author will answer all inquiries accompanied by SASE.

Lamp Design Number	Height	Description
4002	19¾	Lady's face in old-fashioned bonnet, with bow under chin and long streamers - oval base.
4014	22¼	Tall, long-legged pony, oval base (also R-235)
4017	18½	Short pony, long legs, oval base (also R-103)
4034	16¾	Small circle of sparrows on round base
4041	23½	Sphere, with three large plumes at even intervals, round base (also R-281)
4068	28¼	Tall cylinder shape, front cut out - flowers set in cut-out area, round base
4105	17	Globe resting in seaweed base w/fish - oval base
4106	18	Tall narrow handled basket w/flowers - square base
4108	19¾	Stack of books - square base
4110	25	Modernistic lady's head on long neck - sq. step base
4112	18	2-Deer standing, heads-up - rectangular base
4123	18½	Wolfhound standing, tail down, right position, figure eight base (also R-319)
4124	18½	Wolfhound standing, tail down, left position, figure eight base (also R-318)
4127	29	Large upright cornucopia on round base (also R-332B)
4148	15	Camel, neck up, on oval base
4152	23½	3 calla lilies on cylinder, round base
4159	21¾	Peasant man standing, bare to waist, stalk of bananas on his head (also R-403)
4160	23¼	Zebra head and neck on square base - with striped shade
4161	21¾	Peasant woman with basket on head, round base (also R-404)
4162	19	Double racing horses, upward tilt, front legs tucked under, hind legs stretched out, on foliage base. (horses also R-408)
4172	21½	Cabbage roses on small cylinder - round base (also R-377)
4177		Toy soldier
4178		Soldier in different dress
4182	20	Lady's tall boot - oval base
5001	15¼	2-Birds, vertical, perched on cylinder - oval base
5018	20½	Small giraffe on oval base (neck up)
5024	19½	Plume - rect. step-base (also R-248)
5033	18¾	3 small lilies on round base of tall cylinder
5046	20½	2 modern greyhounds on oval base - one with head down - one with head up and turned back (also R-166 & R-167)
5051	20½	Toad stools clustered on round base
5053		Ram's Head, chin down, tightly curled horns - oval base
5058	21½	Pheasant, head and tail up, wings spread and down, round base
5084	24	Double row of lilies on cylinder column - round base
5100		Modernistic lady's head, chin down, banana curls, sq. base
5114	24½	Double horse heads on tall, square pedestal base

5115	19¼	2 lambs playing on rect. base
5116		Leopard on rock, head-up and turned - rect. base (also referred to as "tiger" R-314)
5151		South sea belle (shoulders are base) original shade has large palm leaves (also R-390)
5154		South sea boy (shoulders are base) original shade has large palm leaves (also R-391)
5171	21	Bison on rect. base (See #74 in photo section) (also R-379)
5174	27	Cabbage roses on *large* cylinder - round base
5190		Bronco Buster (cowboy on bucking horse) oval base (also R-424)
5192		Mare and foal, standing, long oval base (also R-451)
5195	24	2 Fawns - one standing - one lying - (right & left positions) oval scalloped base (also R-412 & R-413)
5198		Large giraffe, standing - oval base
5202	25¼	Macaw on limb of tree tunk (also R-425)
5205		Girl on knees, on turtle's back
5220	29	Birds in a cirlce, on top of urn vase, round base
5221	35	Horse head on hitching post (right & left positions)
5222	33	Large ebony head (man), rect. base
5223	23½	Indian head w/"mohawk" hair style, square base
5225	24½	Golf bag, round base
5226	22½	Hawaiian girl resting on torso (for base)
5227	22½	Hawaiian boy resting on torso (for base)
5229	26¼	Dueling pistols, oval base
5230	29	Large fawn heads - round base
5232	24½	Dolphin, resting on chin, tail up and bent
5237		Elephant pin-up lamp
5238		Cornucopia pin-up lamp
5239		Plume pin-up lamp
5240		Horse head and neck pin-up lamp
5242	16/21 adjustable	Large leopard, long rect. base, original shade in leopard print (shade also long & rectangular)
5245	34	Tall square column, butterfly perched on top
5256	41	Cat chorus (double layer of cats on cylinder) round base
5260	20	Small mongolian lady - round base (also R-673)
5261	20	Small mongolian man - round base (also R-672)
5265	23	Squirrels playing
5275	16	Buffalo desk lamp (shade and upright tubes of polished copper) fluorescent light, long rect. base (R-379)
5286X	38	Imperial mongolian woman - round base (also R-634)
5285	35	Imperial mongolian man - round base (also R-633)
5289	25	Large polar bear w/2 babies, long rect. base
5290		Gondola w/gondolier - long base w/long sq. shade (also R-657)
5292	26	3-Plumes on square step base
5303	43	Fishes on waved column
5304	21	Panther and young
5305		3-Roman horse heads in a row, wavey base
5306	30	Running deer, oval base (also R-706)
5307	30	Standing deer, oval base (also R-707)
5311		Panther, left position, long rect. base (original shade is leopard print)
5316		Birds in clouds (tall vertical square for base)
5322	26	Ram's head, chin down, horns curled loosely, square pedestal base
5323		Chess horse head on round pedestal base (original shade: black/white curved stripes)
5324X		Chinese man - hem of kimono makes round base
5325X		Chinese lady - hem of kimono makes round base
5328		Prospector on mule w/baskets (also R-479)
5330		Buddha, sitting position (also R-694)
5331		Indian on horse w/cactus, oval base (also R-721)

5333		Ming horse, rect. base (also R-720)
5336		Horse and colt heads on oval base (also R-739)
5337		Giraffe and young, heads and necks, oval base (also R-740)
5338		Temple goddess on round pedestal base (also R-759)
5351		Flying fish on wave, original shade - large print foliage
5363		Frog and leaves, original shade - large print leaves
5378	25	Gazelle planter/lamp, (also R-869)
5380	25¼	2 tall goose quills, on end, round base
5381	34	Octopus, round in shape, with many curly tenacles
5382	36	Large pineapple for base
5388	23	Fighting cock, head down, tail up and over back (also R-790)
5389	23	Fighting cock, head up, resting on tail-folded under for base (also R-791)
5398	23	Mermaid sitting on wave base
5421	22	Anchor abstract, anchor forms base
5427	24	Birds frolicking among semi-tropical leaves
5433	25	Leaping colt, planter/lamp
5437	27	Flying duck, wings up and together over head (also R-840)
5438	27	Setting duck, wings up and open
5469	35	Giraffe standing, long legs, neck and head turned toward back, modern styling
5481	24¼	Double racing hoses, straight out, on long oval foliage base. (also R 408)
6007	30½	Aquatic trio, 3 sunfish on wavey cylinder, round base
6008	31	Tall swan, neck and head on breast, tail up over head, round base
6010	29½	Tall pagoda base
6011	31¼	Abstract man
6012	31½	Abstract woman
6014	30¼	Tribal mask man, square base
6015	30¼	Tribal mask woman, square base
6018	28	Heaven's gate (tall, square base with opening oriental overtones)
6019	31½	Cockatoo on stump
6020	29½	Girl on clouds (nude figural standing on cloud-like base)
6021	29½	Neptune on sailfish, left position (R-1177)
6022	29½	Mermaid on sailfish, right position (R-1178)
6023	26	Garden girl, sitting with basket and large straw hat, oval base, (also S 230 & R-1179)
6032	25½	Peasant man, head down, square base (also R-382)
6033	32½	Peasant woman, basket on hip, square base (also R-383)
6051	6	Panther, right position, curved shield behind, long oval base (panther 13") (also R-733)
6055	30	Smiling player's mask
6072	22	Wagon wheel on square base
6073	23	Water pump w/bucket on rect. base
6078	29½	Large pinecone for base
6079	19	Goat with cart planter/lamp
6104	23½	Large elephant w/planter, trunk up, standing on all four legs
6106	32	Roman helmet on square pedestal base
6141	20	Horseshoe resting on curved part, ends up wrought iron 4-leg base
6142	28½	Rooster head, large
6143	18	Cannon, rect. base
6144	26½	Giraffe & young, full bodies, reclining on rect. base (also R-1301)
6147	26	Doe & young, full bodies, reclining on rect. base (also R-1296)
6159	30½	"Joy of Life" figurine - girl standing, arms outstretched, scarves trailing to ground, forming base
6169	26½	Girl and fawn running - both have legs outstretched running thru tall grass, girl's hair swept back, oval pedestal base
6172	19½	Sitting girl and fawn planter, long rect. base
6174	30¼	Shot gun for base (pheasants on shade)

6195	30¼	Fish and sea gull, round base
6204	30	Stallion head, head up and forward, tall round pedestal base
6234	30½	"Thunder & Lightning" (3 horses, at different heights, leaping thru zig-zag lightning bolt, long rect. base) (Also: R-1407)
6248	22	Boxer reclining, ashtray/lamp combo, semi-circle base (also: R-1396)
6262	27-¾	Large ming tree, round base
6278	33½	Hibiscus on large cylinder, round base
6279	31	Flying duck on wave-like foliage, wings half, (right and left positions)
6281	29½	Nude girl on dolphin's back (Also: R-363)
6282	22	Poodle sitting, ashtray/lamp combo, semi-circle base R-1440)
6283	22	Cocker standing, ashtray/lamp combo, semi-circle base (R-1442)
6291	23	Sunfish on wave, (base is wave)
6297	27	Modern rooster standing proud, cut-outs in tail (right and left positions)
6342	28	"El Toro" bull lamp, accompanied by #6343 matador figurine in Haeger red-11½"

We have been told that often lamp numbers represented the year and design number. Such as #6342 would indicate the year 1963 and design number 42.

BETTER HOMES & GARDEN MAGAZINE - 1947

Color and Beauty . . . For your library or living room . . . this Haeger lamp, ash tray and pipe combination, are in exquisite taste. The set is glazed in beautiful blending shades of amber and complementary red bronze. Lamp is 21½ inches high with Glastron shade. The set, $31.00. Available now at leading dealers everywhere.

ROYAL HAEGER LAMP CO., INC., 7 MAIDEN LANE, DUNDEE, ILL.

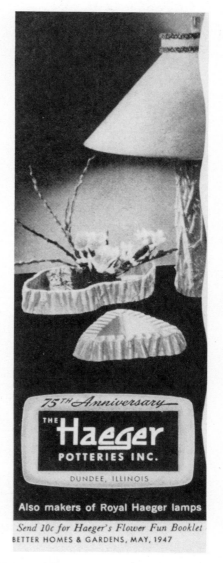

75TH *Anniversary*

THE **Haeger** POTTERIES INC.

DUNDEE, ILLINOIS

Also makers of Royal Haeger lamps

Send 10c for Haeger's Flower Fun Booklet

BETTER HOMES & GARDENS, MAY, 1947

Royal Haeger lamp ads from 1947 *Better Homes & Gardens* magazines.

Ad from October, 1951 *Better Homes & Gardens*

Ad from April, 1952 *Better Homes & Gardens*

You can "re-do" most any room beautifully with

Haeger

That's right! . . . brighten it up with new colors; give it a brand new look with the right new lamps; and related new artwares—and be sure they're *right*—choose Haeger—for generations *the great name in American ceramics.*

You'll be surprised at how little it costs

Choose for your bright new look from the Haeger galaxy of designs— in today's best colors in authentic interpretations of Country Casual, Contemporary, Far East, or whatever best suits your project. And you'll discover that Haeger for all its colorful beauty and originality *never hampers good taste with high cost.*

At good retailers nationwide.

HAEGER POTTERIES, INC.
7 MAIDEN LANE · DUNDEE, ILL.

Furniture by Heritage
Photo Nowell Ward

From *House Beautiful*, April, 1962

The *difference is made by*

Haeger Ceramics

SALLY POTTER says: "A husband never hides behind the paper in this arrangement!"

GET HIM IN A CORNER. Don't get the mopes if you can't afford to "re-do" your living room. You can lift it out of the doldrums . . . make it look entirely different . . . make "him" look at you with new admiration—

IN YOUR "MR. AND MRS." ARRANGEMENT. Your home revolves around you two, doesn't it! Then why not arrange furniture and accessories for the *companionable* leisure of "Mr. and Mrs."?

ARE YOU "APPLES IN A BOWL" TRADITIONAL? Then you'll just naturally reach for an apple as you settle comfortably under the light of this magnificent lamp.

—OR RANCH HOUSE MODERN? Here you see the same furniture, but, obviously, a different family lives here. Amazing, isn't it, how clearly that *entire change in personality* is expressed with Haeger Ceramics.

NOW, LET YOURSELF GO! If your floor space is limited, this corner arrangement will make the room seem larger. In a spacious room try "two chairs and a table" away from the wall. Be certain, in either case, that your chairs are comfortable and your table a convenient height. Then you are ready to give your "Mr. and Mrs." arrangement individuality and personality through your selection of Haeger Ceramics.

At your favorite store featuring Haeger Ceramics you'll find just the lamp you want . . . engineered for good reading. You'll find it in the colors you want, in a brilliant gloss, a satin glaze or a rich new pewter effect. You'll find ashtrays, bowls, vases, figurines in countless designs, colors, glazes and you'll always be proud of your selection, for Haeger is the great name in American Ceramics.

Cordially,

Sally Potter

Director Home Service Division

The Haeger *Potteries,* INC. 7 MAIDEN LANE · DUNDEE, ILLINOIS

Product information for your convenience
Modern accessories; lamp 5463, bowl R814, cigarette boxes and ashtrays R685 and R686. Table by Sterling Furniture Inc.; chairs by Stratford Furniture Corp.

TRADITIONAL

MODERN

Traditional accessories; lamp 5458, bowl R866, pipe and tray RM811, smoking set R863 and R864. Table by Sterling Furniture Inc.; chairs by Stratford Furniture Co.

— 93 —

TV Lamps and TV Lamp/Planter Combinations

The flamboyant and fabulous era of the '50s brought many changes in our lives! Television was here to stay! An entirely new concept in lighting was needed! As the sets came into our living-rooms, we were told: "a light on top was a *must* in order not to ruin our eyes." Hence - the birth of TV lamps.

Royal Haeger TV lamps enjoyed a successful run. In researching these lamps, many were found to have raised lettering on the bottom, with an "R" prefix and number - others had just the label affixed. Many of the figurines introduced in the Royal Haeger line were used as the basis of the TV lamp, with necessary modifications being made. (This will help to recognize a Haeger TV lamp combination).

A partial listing and description of the TV lamps follows. Also, several examples are shown in the photo section of the Guide.

Design No. for TV Lamp	Height	Description
5353	11¼	Petal louvre TV and/or reflector lamp
5415	14	Gazelle TV/planter (R-809)
5430		Pearl shell TV, tall (R-887)
5434	8	Resting stag TV/planter (R-880)
5442	11	Double horse TV/planter, galloping, hind legs out (R-883)
5452	12½	Abstract fish (3 fish - 3 waves) (R-157)
5472	11¼	Swan louvre TV, neck down, tail up (R-856)
5473	15¼	2-Deer abstract TV - one sanding with head up, other with head down (R-1171)
5476	9	Oriental mask TV planter
5488	10	Doe head reflector lamp
6036	7	Comedy & tragedy masks TV lamp (R-1170)
6039	6¼	Gazelle TV/planter, art deco semi-circle style (R-1351)
6043	13¼	Double angel-fish TV lamp
6044	11	Prancing horse TV/planter (R-1262) & (S-229)
6051	6	13" Panther with shield behind, on long oval base (R-733)
6053	10¼	Running stag TV/planter (R-975)
6067	18¼	Mermaid TV lamp
6069	14	Rooster TV planter leg curled up, tail with cut-outs
6086	15	Peacock TV lamp, tail up and spread out (R-31)
6105	11½	Bronco TV/planter (R-1239)
6110	13¼	Pegasus louvre light, cone shape (TV and/or reflector light)
6116	7	Acanthus TV/planter lamp
6118	9¾	Double fish on circular wave TV lamp
6124	13¼	Fish w/beautiful fins and long tail, swimming through seaweed - TV lamp/planter
6140	8¼	Sailfish curled around wave TV lamp (R-1191)
6193	13¼	Colt TV lamp/planter, head on chest, front legs up, hind legs stretched out
6198	7¼	Gondola TV/planter, half-moon shield behind (R-657)
6199	13	Diana & fawn TV/planter - both running in foliage
6200	10½	Gazelle TV lamp/planter, long horns back, front legs up, hind legs stretched out
6202	10¼	Greyhound TV lamp/planter (stretched out, running)
6263	9½	Globe reflector TV lamp, wrought iron legs
6289	13	Bell flower TV lamp
6301	12	Freeform lantern TV/planter
6302	16	2-Stag TV/planter, one standing, one sitting
6322	21½	Ocean fantasy TV lamp, 3 angel-fish (at different heights) on 3 modernistic waves (at different heights).
6341	10¼	Cocker TV/reflector lamp for mantel (R-1442)
6356	10¼	Poodle TV/reflector lamp for mantel (R-1440)
6357	10½	Boxer TV/reflector lamp for mantel (R-1396)

In 1971 during the 100th anniversary year of The Haeger Potteries, Inc., a division of German's famed W. Goebel Company was licensed (for a short period of time) to produce Royal Haeger Lamps for the European market.

Collectors who suffer from "Hummelmania" will be interested to know that Goebel and Haeger celebrated their 100th anniversary simultaneously. In an exchange of gifts, Goebel presented Haeger Potteries with the second largest Hummel figurine ever made. This figure, "Merry Wanderer" is on display at the Haeger Museum in Dundee, Illinois.

Dinnerware

Although dinnerware is not always under the "Royal Haeger" label, as a service to our readers (and for collectors of children's dishes), we take this opportunity to touch briefly on the subject. The following is an excerpt written by Jo Cunningham:

Surprising to many, Haeger had a dinnerware line as early as 1919. This line was simply referred to as 'tableware' and included pieces such as hexagonal plates, salad bowls with matching salad plates, and mayonnaise bowl. Haeger had another line referred to as 'Teaware' and that line included various styles of teapots, creamers, sugars, teacups, saucers, trays and mixing bowls. A child's feeding set - made up of a baby plate, cereal bowl, pitcher, mug and plate - was also manufactured. The children's line came in white with a hand applied lithograph of a baby chick perched next to its eggshell. The baby plate had a litho of two Dutch children playing with geese.

Haeger's 1927 catalog shows a No. 72 teapot and tile, hot water pitcher, sugar and creamer in a 'rich semi-mat black.'

A late 1920s and early 1930s Haeger price list had available an individual breakfast set, a mocha set, three different tea sets, an individual tea set, an iced tea set, salad set, punch sets, fruit set, all furnished in three colors: amarillo, chinese blue, and mergreen. A dresser set was offered in amarillo.

The early Haeger dinnerware was offered in rich blue, yellow and green. A large variety of pieces was offered in a Marshall-Field's brochure from about 1929/1933. Some of the shapes are slightly reminiscent of Homer Laughlin's 'Riviera' by almost ten years.

A stoneware dinnerware line was introduced by Haeger in the 1970s but because Haeger was primarily an artware plant, they could not produce the dinnerware as competitively as needed."

HAEGER POTTERY

MARSHALL FIELD & COMPANY

LET Haeger Pottery bring color to your table! Haeger Pottery—the colorful and beautifully shaped tea ware that is surprisingly inexpensive and easily and quickly obtainable because it is a local product. A complete range of modern shapes for various entertaining purposes comes in four colors—blue, rose, yellow and green. Fineness of glaze and unusual durability make it appropriate and practical for breakfast, luncheon, tea and dinner—indoors and out! It makes a welcome gift to every home — and selection is simplified by the illustrated list inside. Just call or write to our China Section and ask for the pieces, shapes, and colors you want. Haeger Pottery will become an indispensable charm in your home!

China Section, Second Floor

1929-1933

OVENPROOF STONEWARE — BURNT ORANGE SANDSTONE
by Ben Seibel

3206 Warmer
6" x 3"

3210
7" Casserole

3205
Covered
Casserole
10" x 3½"

3212 Salad Bowl
10" x 3½"

3213 Salad Bowl
7" x 2½"

3208 Baking Dish
8½" x 13"

3212

Pitcher
Ht. 6½"

3207
Snack Tray 10" x 7"

3209 Baking Dish
6½" x 10"

3215 Pepper
Ht. 4"

3214 Salt

Mug

3211 Covered Ramekin
Dia. 5"

Additional Colors

Flambe - A number of Haeger glazes are blends of two or more colors and are best described by the French word "flambe" which means "flamed".

Cats Eye - A combined color resembling closely the whitish-green of the cats eye gem. It is a most attractive color and much in demand.

Blue of Sky - A dark blue covered with a blending white in such a way as to give a cloudy effect.

Green and Agate Blue - A medium green blending into a white and blue flambe. The green and blue predominate in the blend.

Chinese Blue - A dark blue sometimes speckled with darker powdered flakes.

Geranium Leaf Green - A light green of soft, velvety appearance which suggests the texture and color of a geranium leaf.

Artware

Haeger...Craftsmen for over a century

5008H-10"

3203/8244 Set
8 Qt. Tureen - Ht. 10"

3196-15"

3199X-8"

8241
8½"x12"

8243
14"x6"

4221-11"
12 Cup

4210-9½"

8239-17"   WHOLE WHEAT

8231-11"

3202
8"x7"x2"

2119-6"

3201 Set

8238-11½"

3200-4"

4220-3½"

8236-7"   8235-9"   8234-11"   4212-12 oz.   4213-22 oz.

"Country Classics" in STONEWARE... a hand decorated tabletop collection in Early American tradition, designed for refrigerator-to-oven-to-table versatility. Ovenproof, chip resistant, and dishwasher safe. Illustrated here in Taupe with a motif chosen especially for our bicentennial year.

Royal Haeger Rarities

Listed below are some magnificent designs, considered rare and hard to find:

1. Designer Eric Olsen's red bull, 8″ x 18″ long (label only). Designer Royal Hickman's black panther (tail stretched out) R-495, 26″ long.

2. Rudolph the Red-Nose Reindeer (lamp base and/or planter). This delightful 1949 personaltiy is numbered R-766. (Picture in photo section #70).

3. "Royal Haeger Award - First Place Prize - 1947 B. Segal". In 1947, as part of Haeger's 75th Anniversary celebration, a national ceramic design competition was initiated by the pottery. The Awards were opened to ceramists and artists through the United States.

4. A recent visit to Janesville, Wisconsin (former home of Parker Pen Company) turned up the gold Parker Pen holder. This Hickman design is in the shape of a semi-circle, with a fluted outer edge.

5. Royal Haeger's 1941 line included some very special Portable Electric Fountains. (See Figure 22). These fountains were connected in the same manner as a table lamp, using ordinary A.C. current and recycled the same water:

   Model #8010 - 20″ bowl with 3 mermaid flower frog-over pump. (Picture #73 in Photo Section).
   #8030 - 20″ bowl with boy and watering can-over pump
   #8040 - 20″ bowl with nude on turtle's back-over pump
   #8050 - 15″ bowl with bird flower block-over pump

   (Known colors: Satin White, Musty Grey, Alice Blue)

6. In addition to Haeger's fountains, they also included a line of music box pieces. (See Figure 23 and Figure 24).
   A. Musical cradle, #613, played "Rock-A-Bye Baby"
   B. Musical cradle, #3348 played "Rock-A-Bye Baby"
   (See: Picture #67 in the photo section)
   The cradles came in satin white, baby pink and baby blue.
   C. Musical vase, #3043, played "Happy Birthday to You"
   D. Musical vase, #3417, played "Happy Birthday to You" (satin white only).
   E. Musical madonna, #3427, played "Ave Marie"
   F. Musical madonna, #3927, played "Silent Night"

   Each of the above-listed designs contained a Swiss musical instrument concealed on the underside of the piece, with a control lever to start and stop the music.

7. Haeger did make a few decorative clocks, and this author is lucky enough to own one! Clock #601 is a combination planter, pen holder, and clock on a square base. The base is 8½″ x 4½″, and the cornucopia styling which holds the clock in one end, holds flowers in the other, with an overall measurement of 13¼″. (See: Picture #30 in photo section).

   The only other clock seen to date, is in the Haeger Museum at Dundee, Illinois. This clock is free standing, as well as coming with a matching wall shelf for hanging. This lovely 2-pc. set is done in ebony, trimmed with small flowers, and edged with gold.

Randall's Portable Electric Fountains

Sold only through Florists. You can sell these to other shops for display purposes as well as to your customers for home use.

Ready for prompt shipment from Chicago stock.

Randall Portable Electric Fountains

Randall Portable Electric Fountains now equipped with our marvelous fool-proof motor.

The pottery bowls and centerpieces have been designed for us by Haeger Potteries, and are of fine quality and highly decorative. With our guarantee of satisfactory performance you can whole-heartedly recommend these fountains to those of your customers who appreciate the unusual. They are available in Alice Blue and Gloss White.

The fountains are electrically operated—connect as you would a table lamp. Portable—no plumbing connections required—uses same water over and over again. Center figure completely conceals pumping unit. Moisture will not harm motor—may be operated continuously without harm even if bowl should run dry. Requires ordinary A. C. current, 110 to 120 volts, 60 cycles. Equipped with connecting cord—simple to operate.

Randall Fountain No. 8070
Complete, Flowers Excluded
$19.50
Diameter 17"
Height 8"

Colors
Gloss White
Alice Blue

Randall Fountain No. 8030
Complete, Flowers Excluded
$25.00
Diameter 12" x 20"
Height 13"

F.O.B. CHICAGO, ILL.

Arrangements by "Tommy" Bright

Page 64 • A. L. RANDALL COMPANY, 1433 South Wabash Avenue, CHICAGO 5, ILLINOIS

Figure 22. From *Randall's Catalog,* July, 1950.

Musical Cradles—by Haeger

Haeger Musical Cradles always receive favorable comment, not only from the new mother, but from her friends. It is only natural that our sales on musical cradles continue to increase.

No. 3348 Haeger Musical Cradle. Each **$2.75**
Length 8", Width 4", Height 6"
Colors: Satin White, Baby Pink, Baby Blue

The Swiss musical instrument used is sturdy in construction and of fine quality. It should last for many years.

A small lever starts and stops the music at will.

No. 613 Haeger Musical Cradle. Each **$2.50**
Length 5½", Width 3½", Height 4"
Colors: Satin White, Baby Pink, Baby Blue

Arrangements by Bright's School of Design

A. L. RANDALL COMPANY, 1433 South Wabash Avenue, CHICAGO 5, ILLINOIS • Page 17

Figure 23. From *Randall's Catalog*, July, 1950.

Flowers With Music

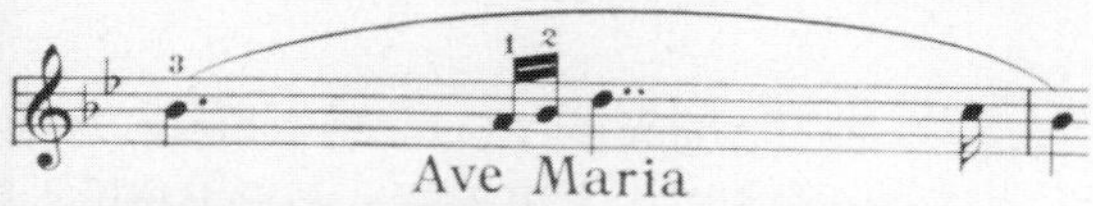

Ave Maria

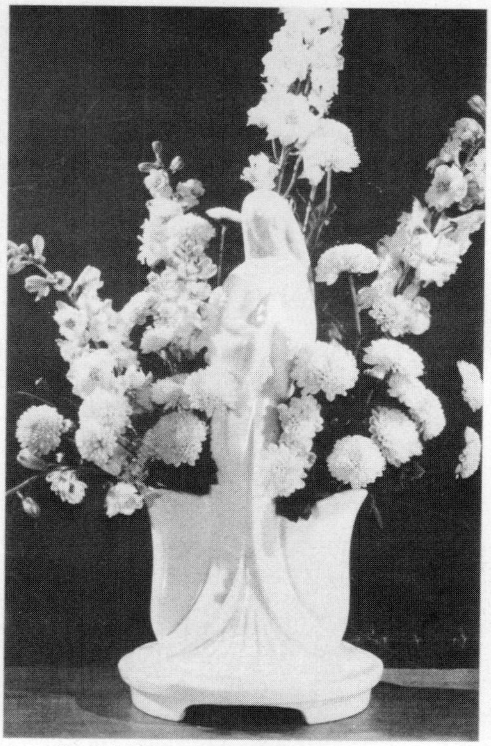

Our records show that these lovely Musical Madonna Vases sell the year around. The heaviest demand is for Christmas and Easter. For Christmas sales we offer a choice of instruments playing "Ave Maria" or "Silent Night". Please express your preference when ordering.

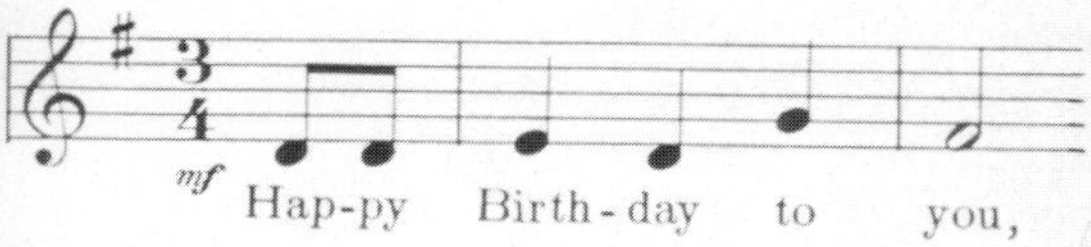

Hap-py Birth-day to you,

No. 3427 Haeger Musical Madonna. Each $3.75
Overall Height 11½". Compartment Height 3¾"
Opening 4½" x 2"

Color: Satin White Only

3427AM Ave Marie
3927SN Silent Night

Some birthdays seem to demand something unusual. Our Musical Birthday Vase fits such occasions beautifully. The musical instrument concealed in the base plays "Happy Birthday To You". There is a control lever to start and stop the music.

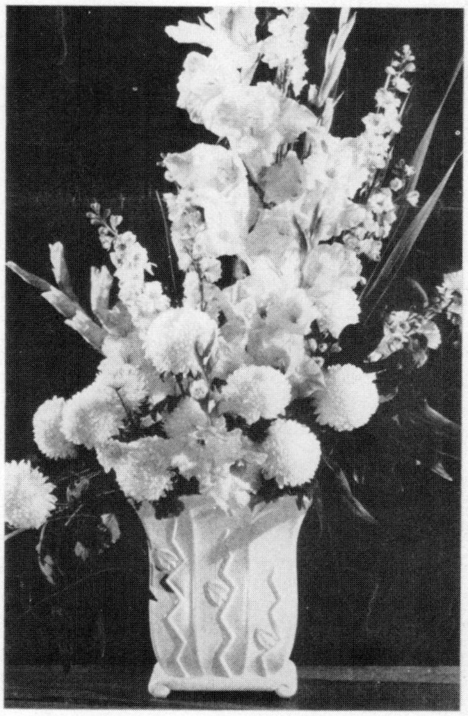

No. 3417 Haeger Musical Birthday Vase. Each $3.25
Height 8", Opening 6" x 4"

Color: Satin White Only

Arrangements by "Tommy" Bright
Photos by Kistler

Figure 24. From *Randall's Catalog*, July, 1950.

Commemorative and Advertising Items

The commemorative and advertising pieces (as with the dishes) are not all under the Royal Haeger label - some are from the regular Haeger line. However, we take this opportunity to present to our readers a brief sampling of these pieces.

Designs of this nature with advertising or depicting a certain time or event are always important to any collection - as they are generally a "one-time" issue.

1. Set of 4 Sesquicentennial Ashtrays (Illinois 1818-1968)
   a. Lincoln profile in relief #1095
   b. Stephen A. Douglas, in relief #1096
   c. Jane Addams, in relief #1098
   d. Louis Joliet, in relief #1097 (missing from photo)
   (See: Picture #108 in photo section).

2. Ashtray 4½ x 4½ - "Haeger 1871/1971 Craftsmen for a Century" (See Picture #90 in photo section).

3. Ashtray, round, with raised crown in the center and lettering: "Say It With Flowers In A Haeger Container" (See: Picture #107 in photo section).

4. Ashtray, 5½" lettering: "Cook-Heat Electrically 1958 McDonough Power Cooperative" (See: Picture #107 in photo section).

5. Shape of Illinois ashtray, lettering: "Midwest Tool Collectors Association, 1982" . . .R-1892S.

6. Ashtray, round, lettering: "Spirit of '76, Randall Creations for A Beautiful America" (See: Picture #109 in photo section).

7. Ashtray, round, lettering: "Haeger Potteries-Over A Century of Craftsmanship".

8. Shape of Illinois ashtray, Lincoln's Head in relief: "Land of Lincoln" . . . R-1892S (See: Picture #108 in photo section).

9. Shape of Michigan ashtray, bridge pictured, lettering: "The World's Longest Suspension Bridge" . . .R-1856 (See: Picture #60 in photo section).

10. Shape of Illinois ashtray, lettering: "Western Illinois University - Macomb" (See: Picture #76 in photo section).

11. Shape of Maine ashtray, lettering "Maine Lions" showing raised figure of lion.

12. Shape of Texas ashtray, raided design of: star, cowboy, hat, cacti, oil well and "Texas" letters. (R-1858)

13. Cookie jar, 2 pc. matte white, shaped like a pig, lettering: "Bartlow Brothers, Inc. Korn Top".

14. Old Sleepy Eye Commemoratives:
    a. Oval brown disk for the Collectors' Club, Macomb, Illinois, July 27-28, 1979 . . .#171, #222, & #159.
    b. Round plate, royal blue, for Collector's Club, Macomb, Illinois, July 28-29, 1978 . . .#588. Items a & b were seen recently at APEC priced: $200.00-250.00 ea.

15. Cookie jar with "Keebler Elf" in front of tree trunk, with green foliage for top of jar. (Haeger Museum) * Haeger did the original cookie jar, but it was later done by Nelson McCoy. One of the main differences in the jars is the little man was hand-painted by Haeger, and McCoy used a decal.

16. Cornucopia on pedestal (aladdin lamp styling) with "1934 A Century of Progress" Chicago World's Fair label. Haegerware made and sold on this site, bear this special mark. (See: Page 64 for an example of this label, and Photo #77 in the photo section).

Decanters

Another most desirable treasure for the Royal Haeger collector would be the Ezra Brooks Ceramic Decanters. Jerry Adler, executive vice-president of Medley Distilling Company, has this to say:

"At one time this was a major acitivity for us. There were Collector Clubs around the country, a newsletter for collectors, and new ceramic releases.
But time and events change, and as a consequence of a declining market for collector ceramics, we were obliged to discontinue the operations of the Ezra Brooks Ceramic Company two years ago.
Although Haeger did not make all the Ezra Brooks decanters, they did make the following:

Gavel Gift Box - Wood Block 200ml
President Ceramic Gavel (2 feet high) 750 ml
Chairman Ceramic Gavel (3 feet high) 1.75 liter
Washington Monument
Pontiac Race Car
Pontiac Black Special
Pontiac Indy Pace Car 1980
Illinois American Legion 1983
King Tut Shrine Guard

Shrine - Sphinx
1.75 Historical Jug #2
F.O.E. (Fraternal Order of Eagles)

The name Heritage was created by Ezra Brooks.

The letter "H" on the bottom of the Ezra Brooks decanters was our symbol that appeared on all bottles. It had no reference to Haeger" . . .

(Jan. 1986)

Other decanters on display at the Museum in Dundee are:

1. Bucky Badger Hockey Player
2. Balloon Clown
3. Porpoise decanter honoring Amvets - Korea/Vietnam
4. Southern California Trojan Horse
5. Harley-Davidson motorcylce (piggy-bank)
6. Bronco Buster
7. Barn Owl (wearing white hat)
8. Water Tower in Chicago
9. Sphinx

Photo Section

Pricing Information

Through our travels, correspondence, purchases, much research, and sharing with other Royal Haeger collectors, we have obtained the knowledge to establish FAIR current market prices for the Royal Haeger collectibles.

Of course, the Guide is intended to be just that - a Guide. Many things that would govern the seller's price choice, as well as the buyer's, would be known only to them. When no condition is indicated, the prices are for pieces in "mint" condition.

With regard to categories such as: Dinnerware, Decanters, and Studio Haeger, we can in no way establish a fair market price, as so few pieces have been available for collecting. Designs in these categories are scarce and desirable!

In the photo section, when a design is marked "PND" - it indicates no price has been established. These Haeger rarities are seldom seen and with only a few being made, rather than guess at their value - we have marked them PND. From this Photo Section, ONLY the designs with an "R" prefix will be listed in the Numerical Index.

Photo 1. #5195, 2-Fawn Lamps, pr. (right & left positions), 24″h, $30.00-35.00 ea. #5174, Cabbage Rose Lamp, 24″h, $25.00-30.00.

Photo 2. #R-426, Cornucopia Vase w/nude, 8″h, $15.00-18.00. Label, Cylinder Lamp w/small Dappled Horse, 25″h, $30.00-35.00.#R-287, Wren House w/2 Birds, 9½″h, $12.00-15.00.

Photo 3. #R-713, Swan Vase, 8″h, $10.00-12.00. #R-271, Sailfish Vase, ″h, $20.00-22.00. #R-430, Swan Vase, ″h, $8.00-10.00.

Photo 4. #R-299, Snail Shell Vase, 11″l, $10.00-12.00. #R-31, Peacock Gladiola Vase, (head turned), 15″h, $40.00-45.00. #R-364, Nude Figurine on Seal Block, 13″h $25.00-30.00. #R-224, Daisy Bowl, 12″w, $12.00-15.00.

Photo 5. #R-310, Large Swan, open back, 13″l, $15.00-18.00. #R-281, Sphere w/3 Plume, 10″h, $25.00-30.00. #R-108, Pouter Pigeon, 12″l, $18.00-20.00.

Photo 6. #R-361, 3 Birds-on-Branch lock, 7″l, $10.00-15.00. #R-31, eacock Gladiola Vase, (head straight), 5″h, $40.00-45.00. #R-712, Bird of aradise, small, 9″h $15.00-18.00.

Photo 7. #R-321, Conch Shell Vase, pr., 8″h, $8.00-10.00 ea. R-322, Double Conch Shell Vase/Planter, 7½″l, $15.00-18.00.

Photo 8. #R-182R, Swan Vase (right position), 8″h, $10.00-12.00. #R-33, Large 3-leaf Vase, 13½″h, $20.00-25.00. #R-277, Small Spiral Plume Dish, 6″w, $8.00-10.00.

Photo 9. #R-303, Laurel Wreath Bow Vase, 12″h, $15.00-18.00. #R-29, Violin Bowl planter, 17″l, $12.00-14.00. #R-182L, Swan Vase (left position), 8″h, $10.00-12.00.

Photo 10. #R-312, Cornucopia Candleholders, 5½"h, $4.00-6.00 ea. #R-127, Large round bowl w/floral scalloped top and cut-outs, 13½"w, $25.00-30.00.

Photo 11. #R-386, Basket Vase, 12"l, $15.00-18.00. #R-286, Leaf Plate, 12"l $8.00-10.00.

Photo 12. #F-16, Wild Goose, wings-half, 8"l, $6.00-8.00. #R-186, Bird of Paradise Vase, 13"h, $20.00-25.00. F-17, Wild Goose, wings-up, 8"l, $6.00-8.00.

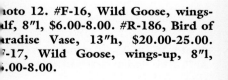

Photo 13. #RG-5, Rectangular Bowl, pink, 9½"l, $3.00-4.00. #RG-68, Bottle Vases, pink & white, blue w/gold tweed & blue w/navy, 7"h, $2.00-4.00. #RG-64, "Leaf" Bowl, yellow, 14"l, $3.00-4.00. #RG-73, S Curve Bowl, white, 14"l, $3.00-4.00. #RG-51, Oval Bowl, cinna brown, 11"l, $3.00-4.00. #RG-42, Pitcher, dark green, 10"h, $6.00-8.00.

Photo 14. #454N, Pig Planter w/gold trim, 10"l, $15.00-18.00. #R-819. Acanthus Console Bowl. 14"l, $8.00-10.00. #R1285, Candleholder, single, 5"l, $4.00-6.00 ea.

Photo 15. *HAEGER logo, PND. #612, Rooster, 12"h, $15.00-20.00. #613, Hen, 10½"h, $15.00-20.00

Photo 16. #505, Mermaid, reclining 21"l, (this design comes in a smaller version), $25.00-30.00.

Photo 17. #R-130, Pheasants, pr., 12″l, $10.00-12.00 ea. *#R-256, Large Jardiniere (Royal Haeger by Royal Hickman), 12″d, PND.

Photo 18. #R-452, Morning Glory Vase, pr., 16″h, $20.00-22.00 ea. #R-422, Cornucopia Vase, small, 6″h, $7.00-9.00.

Photo 19. #R-235, Colt Flower Holder, 12½″h, $20.00-22.00. #R-271. Sailfish Vase, 9″h, $20.00-22.00. #R-714, Fan Vase, 9¼″l, $6.00-8.00.

Photo 20. #3504, Hanging Pot w/chain, 3½″w, $4.00-5.00. #R-36, Swan Vase, tall, 16″h, $35.00-40.00. #R-321, Conch Shell Vase, 8″h, $8.00-10.00. #R-579, 2 Block Candleholder, 5″l, $4.00-6.00 ea.

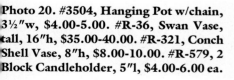

Photo 21. #R-479. Prospector w/burros. 11½″l, $18.00-20.00. #R-776. Sleeping Cocker Pup, 6″l, $6.00-8.00. #R-424. Bucking Bronco w/cowboy, 13″h. $25.00-30.00.

Photo 22. #R-1364. Rococo Bookend, 6″h, $8.00-10.00 ea. #R-1351, Fawn Planter. 17″l, $10.00-15.00. #R-493, Egyptian Cat (head down), 6½″h, $10.00-12.00.

Photo 23. #R-312, Cornucopia Candleholders, 5½″h, $4.00-6.00 ea. #R-466, Long Curving Bowl, 18″l, $6.00-8.00.

Photo 24. #R-1254, Little Brother 11½″h, $15.00-18.00. #R-1179, Garden Girl, sitting, 14″l, (originally S-230) $18.00-22.00

Photo 25. #617, Fawn Planter, 6½″h, $3.00-4.00. #3679, Garden Girl by Pool, 0″h, $18.00-20.00.

Photo 26. #R-816, Petal Bowl w/ebony base, 10½″h, $8.00-10.00. #R-838, Turning Frog Flower block, 4½″h, $10.00-12.00. #R-771, Leaf Bowl, 15″l, $6.00-8.00.

Photo 27. #R-900, Modern Scroll Vase, ″h, $6.00-8.00. #R-987, Basket Vase w/handle, 15½″h, $25.00-30.00. #R-754, Donkey and Cart, 11½″l, 10.00-12.00.

Photo 28. #R-1225, Girl sitting w/
bowls, 13"l, $20.00-25.00. #3528, Dou-
ble Neck Vase, 6"h, $6.00-8.00.

Photo 29. Label, Top Hat - 75th Anniversary Sticker, 3½"h, $6.00-8.00.
#6105, Bronco TV Lamp, 11½"l,
$20.00-25.00. #R-485, Upright
Candleholder (flower & candle combo),
7½"h, 4.00-5.00 ea.

Photo 30. #3237, Standing Deer, 6"h
$2.00-3.00. *#601, Desk Set: electri
clock in cornucopia planter, with pe
holder, 13"l, PND.

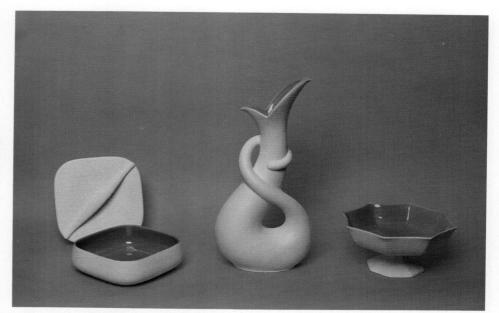

Photo 31. #711S, Square Dish w/lid, 7½″w, $5.00-6.00. #483, "Cobra" vase, 16″h, $10.00-12.00. #3002, Octagon Pedestal Bowl, 8½″w, $4.00-5.00.

Photo 32. #R-1913, "Bambi" deer planter, 7½″h, $10.00-12.00. #138, Ashtray, 8½″l, $4.00-5.00. #507, Cat, sitting (above pcs. are Briar Agate), 8¼″h, $10.00-12.00.

Photo 33. #3377, Scottie Planter, 6″l, $6.00-8.00. #R-1224, Gypsy Girl, standing tall, 16½″h, $30.00-35.00.

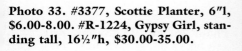

Photo 34. Leaping Gazelle TV Lamp, 13½"l, $20.00-25.00. Fish on Wave Table Lamp, 20"h, $25.00-30.00. #R-301, Leaf Fan Vase, 9½"h, $8.00-10.00

Photo 35. #R-752, Fish Planter, 8½"h, $10.00-12.00. #R-701, Sea Shell Vase, 10¼"h, $12.00-14.00. #R-483, Upright Shell Vase, 11"h, $15.00-18.00.

Photo 36. #R-713, Swans, pair, 7"h, $10.00-12.00 ea. #R-821, Oval Leaf Bowl w/applied fruit, 19"l, $22.00-25.00.

Photo 37. #R-485, Upright Candleholders, pr., 7½"l, $4.00-5.00 ea. #R-363, Nude Astride Fish Block, 10"h, $18.00-20.00. #R-727, Hexagonal Low Bowl, 12"h, $6.00-8.00.

Photo 38. #R-579, 2 Block Candleholder, 5"l, $4.00-6.00 ea. #R-481, Sea Shell on Base, 11"h, $18.00-20.00. #R-476, Beaded Console Bowl, 15"l, $6.00-8.00.

Photo 39. Label, Fawn planter Lamp, 18½"h, $10.00-12.00. #R-412, Standing Fawn, 11½"h, $8.00-10.00. #R-413, Sitting Fawn, 7½"h, $6.00-8.00. #R-560, Cigarette Box w/lid, 7"l, $6.00-9.00.

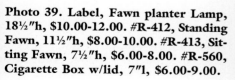

Photo 40. #R-126A, Small Leaf Plate, 11″w, $4.00-6.00. #R-785, Elephant figurine, 5″h, $6.00-8.00. #R-126, Large Leaf Plate, 15″w, $6.00-8.00.

Photo 41. #R-651, Pillow Vase, 8″h, $6.00-8.00. #R-657, Gondolier Planter w/Inserts, 19½″l, $18.00-20.00.

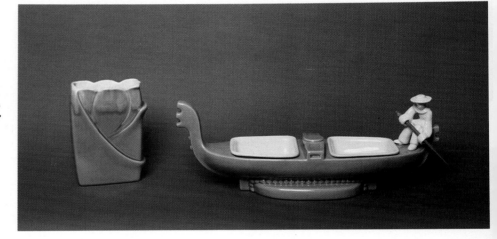

Photo 42. #R-446, Lily Vases, pr., 14″h, $20.00-22.00 ea. #R-364, Nude with Seal Block, 13″h, $25.00-30.00.

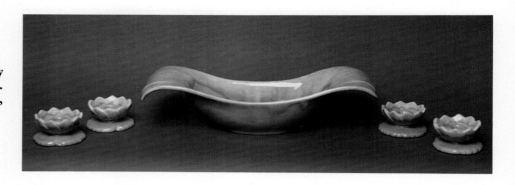

Photo 43. #3288, Water Lily Candleholders, 4"w, $5.00-6.00 ea. #R-370, Dutch Cup Bowl, 19"l, $8.00-10.00.

Photo 44. #1006, Boomerang Ashtray, 12"l, $3.00-4.00. #R-883, Double Racing Horse planter, 11"l, $25.00-30.00.

Photo 45. #R-718, Ram Head Bookends, 5½"h, $18.00-22.00 pr. #R-641, Stallion Bookend planters, 8½"h, $10.00-12.00 ea.

Photo 46. #R-901, Sailfish Vases, small pr., 6"h, $8.00-10.00 ea. #R-907, Lily Pad Leaf bowl, 8"w, $6.00-8.00. Label (R-1458), Vase, small globe, 4½"h, $4.00-6.00.

Photo 47. #R-900, Modern Scroll Vase, 6"h, $6.00-8.00. #3571, Flat Cornucopia, 13"l, $8.00-10.00. #R-757, Hexagon Candleholders, pr, 5"w, $4.00-6.00 ea.

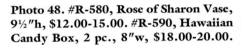

Photo 48. #R-580, Rose of Sharon Vase, 9½"h, $12.00-15.00. #R-590, Hawaiian Candy Box, 2 pc., 8"w, $18.00-20.00.

Photo 49. #R-115, Gazelle Vases, pr, 13"h, $15.00-18.00 ea. #R-628, Chinese Lady, 6"h, $6.00-8.00. #R-629, Chinese Man, 5½"h, $6.00-8.00. #5100, Modern Lady's Head Lamp, 21½"h, $40.00-45.00.

Photo 50. #R-628, Chinese Lady, 6″h, $6.00-8.00. #R-629, Chinese Man, 5½″h, $6.00-8.00. *#R-596, Barnyard Riders, 13¼″h, PND.

Photo 51. #R-426, Cornucopia Vase w/nude, 8″h, $15.00-18.00. #5362, Fluted Ginger Jar Table Lamp, 28″h, $20.00-22.00.

Photo 52. #R-955, Large Swan Console Bowl, 11″h, $18.00-20.00. #R-959, Swan Candleholders, Pr., 5¼″h, $8.00-10.00 ea.

Photo 53. #3108, 2-Deer Abstract Vase, 7″h, $6.00-8.00. #1005, Flower Girl (or Colonial Girl), 7½″h, $6.00-8.00. #3105, Dancing Girl Vase, 8″h, $6.00-8.00. Label, 2-Handled Vase, 9″h, $5.00-7.00. #66, Squirrel Vase, 7½″h, $6.00-8.00.

Photo 54. #R-780, Mr. Scot TV Lamp, 13½″l, $20.00-25.00. Knight's Head, 7″h, $8.00-10.00. #R-736, Dachshund, 14½″l, $18.00-22.00.

Photo 55. #R-733, Panther, 13″l, $12.00-15.00. #R-182L, Swan, 8″h, $10.00-12.00. #R-683, Panther, 18″l, $15.00-20.00.

Photo 56. #R-314X, Tiger Figurine Ebony, 11″h, 30.00-35.00. #R-869 Gazelle Planter, 14″h, $25.00-30.00.

Photo 57. #R-1619S, Pitcher, Ebony Cascade, 16″h, $8.00-10.00. #R-707, Standing Deer Vase, 15″h, 18.00-22.00. #R-990, Turning Stag, ″h, $8.00-10.00. #R-991, Standing tag, 7″h, $8.00-10.00.

Photo 58. #R1531, Standing Colt Vase, 15″h, $20.00-25.00. #408, Handled Pitcher, Tall Thin Neck, Ebony Cascade, 18½″h, $8.00-10.00. #3511, Panther w/white planter, 14½″l, $15.00-20.00.

Photo 59. Comedy & Tragedy TV amp, 9″h, $20.00-25.00. Horse with 'Peg'' Mane, planter, 10″h, 15.00-18.00.

Photo 60. Label, Lady's Head Plante
Art Deco style, 6½"h, $5.00-6.0
#R-1696, Cornucopia, basketweav
18½"l, $15.00-20.00. #R-1856, State
Michigan ashtray, 10"l, $6.00-8.00.

Photo 61. #R-1918, Swan, 10½"l,
$15.00-18.00. #R-351, Squat Urn
w/black base, 10"h, $12.00-15.00.
#R-299, Snail Shell Vase, 7"h,
$10.00-12.00.

Photo 62. #R-299, Snail Shell Vase, 7"
$10.00-12.00. *Haeger Logo PN
#R-1262, Prancing Horse (original
S-229), 11"l, $20.00-25.00.

Photo 63. #R-103, Small Horse, 7″h,
.00-12.00. #5398, Mermaid Table
mp, 26″h, $30.00-35.00. #R-375A,
lar Bear Cub, sitting, 3″h,
.00-8.00. #R-376A, Polar Bear Cub,
nding, 2½″h, $6.00-8.00.

Photo 64. #3278, Eagle Vase, 13″h,
$6.00-8.00. #1974, AMVETS Dolphin
Decanter (Ezra Brooks), 10.00-12.00.
#3268, Art Deco Vase, 7″h, $3.00-4.00.

oto 65. #R-299, Snail Shell Vase, 7″h,
0.00-12.00. #R-363, Nude Astride
h Block, 10″h, $18.00-20.00. #3504,
m for Hanging Pot, 9″h, $8.00-10.00
). #R-132, Ram Bookend, 9″h,
5.00-18.00.

Photo 66. #3232, Double-bran[...] Candleholders, 7"l, $3.00-6.00 [...] #R-298, Cornucopia Shell Vase in pi[...] Boko finish, 11"h, $20.00-22.00.

Photo 67. *#613, Cradle w/Swiss Music Box (plays Rock-a-Bye Baby), 5½"l, PND.

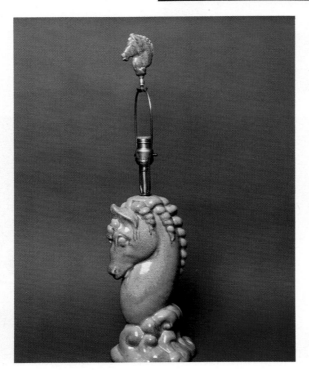

Photo 68. *Horse Head Lamp w/matching finial, 28"h, PND.

Photo 69. #R-386, Basket Vase, 12"l, $15.00-18.00. #R-1225, Girl Sitting w/two bowls, 13"h, $20.00-25.00. #R-426, Cornucopia Vase w/nude, 8"h, $15.00-18.00.

Photo 70. *#R-766, "Rudolph the Red Nose Reindeer, lamp base (also made as a planter), 10"h, PND.

Photo 71. #R-791, Fighting Cock, 11½"h, $20.00-22.00. #6093, Half Moon Planter Lamp, 26"h, $20.00-22.00. #F-16, Wild Goose (wings-half), 7½", $6.00-8.00. #1273, Free Form Ash Bowl, 8"l, $5.00-6.00.

Photo 72. #R-857, Gazelle Head Vase 12″h, $15.00-18.00. #5473, 2-Deer Abstract TV Lamp, 14″h, $20.00-25.00. #R-733, Panther, 13″, $12.00-15.00. #R-649, Lying Leopard, 7″1 $8.00-10.00.

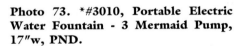

Photo 73. *#3010, Portable Electric Water Fountain - 3 Mermaid Pump, 17″w, PND.

Photo 74. #R-285, Swan Vase, 9″h $10.00-12.00. #5171, Bison Table Lamp w/bird finial, 23½″h, $35.00-40.00. #R-228, Cornucopia Vase, 9″h $15.00-18.00.

Photo 75. #R-299, Snail Shell Vase, 7"h, $10.00-12.00. #5155, Urn Lamp w/black base, 24½"h, $15.00-20.00. #R-284, Trout Vase, 7"h, $15.00-18.00.

Photo 76. Haeger U.S.A., Western Illinois University Ashtray, 10"l, $5.00-6.00. #R-372, Round Fluted Bowl, 13½"w, $8.00-10.00. #R-359, 2-Bird Block, 11"w, $18.00-20.00. #R-301, Fan Vase, dbl. leaf, 9"h, $8.00-10.00.

Photo 77. Label, Tiny Cow Planter (cover of 1938 Better Homes & Garden Magazine), 4½"h, $8.00-10.00. #223C, 2-Handled Jug (Circa 1929), 9½"h, $6.00-8.00. Label, Cornucopia (Aladdin Lamp styling, "Century of Progress - 1934 World's Fair" label), 7"h, $15.00-18.00.

Photo 78. #R-363, Nude Astride Fish Block, 10"h, $18.00-20.00. #R-360, Tropical Fish Block, 11"h $18.00-20.00. #R-820, Bird Block, 7"h, $10.00-15.00.

Photo 79. #R-138, Large Leaf Vases, pr., 12½"h, $10.00-12.00 ea. #R-1146, Stag Planter Art Deco, 5½"h, $8.00-10.00.

Photo 80. #R-287, Wren House, 2 birds, 9½"h, $12.00-15.00.#R-840, Flying Duck Vase, 12"h, $20.00-25.00. #R-904, Setting Duck Vase, 9"h, $15.00-18.00.

Photo 81. #R-595, Trout Pitcher, 8"h, $15.00-18.00. Gazelle TV Lamp, 10½"h, $20.00-25.00. #R-832, Flat Sided Vase w/pearls, 9"h, $10.00-12.00.

Photo 82. #R-228, Cornucopia Vases, pr, 13"h, $15.00-18.00 ea. #R-1455, Small Stag Vase, 4½"h, $6.00-8.00.

Photo 83. #R-647, Sun Flower Vase, 8"h, $8.00-10.00. #R-908, Large Lily Pad Leaf, 11"w, $8.00-10.00. #R-706, Running Deer Vase, 15"h, $18.00-22.00. #R-716, Bud Vase, 9"h, $5.00-8.00. #R-793, Leaf Candleholder, 7"l, $4.00-6.00, ea.

Photo 84. #R-313, Tigress on Rock, Amber Crystal, 9″h. $40.00-45.00.

Photo 85. #R-706, Running Deer Vase, 15″h, $18.00-22.00. #RG-86, Bottle Vase, 7″h, $2.00-3.00. #R-707, Standing Deer Vase, 15″h, $18.00-22.00.

Photo 86. #R-869, Gazelle Planter, 14″h, $25.00-30.00.

Photo 87. #R-646, Tulip Vase, 8″h, $8.00-10.00. Rooster Crowing, 10″h $10.00-12.00. #R-312, Cornucopia Candleholder, 5½″h, $4.00-6.00 ea.

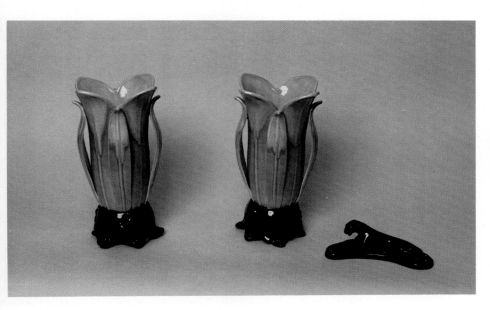

Photo 88. #5353, Petal Louvre Reflector Lamps, ea. 11¼″h, $20.00-25.00. #R-649, Lying Leopard, 7″h, $8.00-10.00.

Photo 89. #483, "Cobra" Vase, 16″h, $10.00-12.00. #R-834, Turtle Planter, 11″l, $15.00-18.00. #R-690, Square Style Chinese Candleholders, 5″w, $5.00-6.00 ea.

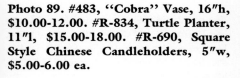

Photo 90. Haeger U.S.A., Commemorative Issue: "Craftsmen for A Century" Ashtray, 4"w, $4.00-6.00. #813-H, Tall Cigarette Lighter, 10½"h, $10.00-12.00. #890, Short Cigarette Lighter, 4½"h, $6.00-8.00. #1006, Boomerang Ashtray, 12"l, $3.00-4.00. *HAEGER gold logo, PND.

Photo 91. #R-713, Swan, 7"h, $10.00-12.00. #3532, Flower Girl w/bowl on lap, 9½"h, $15.00-18.00.

Photo 92. #8259, Sombrero Hat (Hanging Planter), 12"w, $6.00-8.00. #3531, Dancer w/lily base, 9½"h, $8.00-10.00, #R-812, Gondola Planter, 15½"l, $8.00-10.00.

Photo 93. #R-138, Large Leaf Vases, pr, 12½"h, $10.00-12.00 ea. #R-271, Sailfish Vase, 9"h, $20.00-22.00.

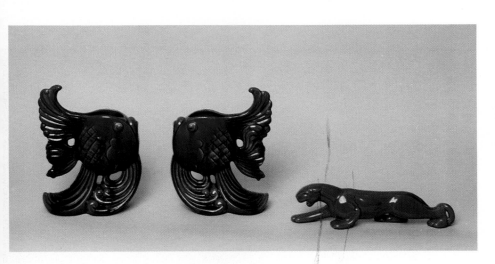

Photo 94. #1240, Moon Fish Planter/Bookends, 10"h, $15.00-20.00 ea. #R-733, Panther, 13"l, $12.00-15.00.

Photo 95. #1919, Bottle Vase, large, 10"h, $4.00-5.00. #RG-68, Bottle Vase, small, 7"h, $2.00-4.00. #408, Handled Pitcher/vase tall thin neck, 18½"h, $8.00-10.00. #483, "Cobra" Vase, 16"h, $10.00-12.00.

Photo 96. #R-407, Wren House w/one bird, 6½"h, $6.00-8.00. #R-364, Nude with Seal Block, 13"h, $25.00-30.00. #R-224, Daisy Bowl, 12"w, $12.00-15.00, #R-301, Double Leaf Fan Vase, 9½"h, $8.00-10.00.

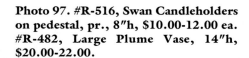

Photo 97. #R-516, Swan Candleholders on pedestal, pr., 8"h, $10.00-12.00 ea. #R-482, Large Plume Vase, 14"h, $20.00-22.00.

Photo 98. #R-485, Upright Candleholder, 7½"l, $4.00-5.00 ea. #R-309, Ruching Bowl, 14½"w, $8.00-10.00. #R-360, Tropical Fish Block, 11"h, $18.00-20.00. #R-10_, Small Horse, 7"h, $9.00-12.00.

Photo 99. #R-312, Cornucopia Candleholders, pr, 5½"h, $4.00-6.00 ea. #R-386, Basket Vase, 12"l, $15.00-18.00.

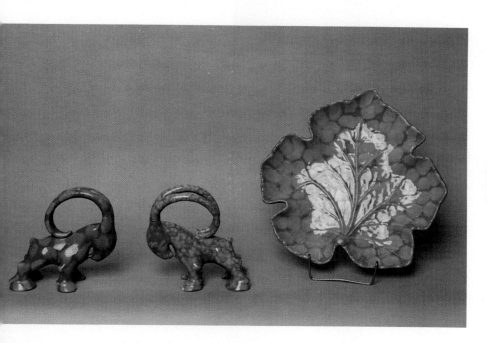

Photo 100. #R-132, Ram Bookends, 9"h, $15.00-18.00 ea. #R-126, Large Leaf Plate, 15"w, $6.00-8.00.

Photo 101. #R-1919, Onion Style Vase, med., 10"h, $4.00-5.00 ea. #481, Swirl Vase, 15"h, $12.00-15.00. #R-1915, Onion Style Vases, pr. (raised, rough finish), 15"h, $8.00-10.00 ea.

Photo 102. #483, "Cobra" Vase, 16"h,
$10.00-12.00. #301-H, Large Shallow
Bowl (pink gold tweed), 14½"w,
$6.00-8.00. #R-1915, Onion Style Vase,
15"h, $8.00-10.00.

Photo 103. (Back Row), Selections from
Junior "All American Series": #B-649,
Stork w/cradle, 6"h, $3.00-4.00; Boy
w/flowers, 6"h, $3.00-4.00; Pair Large
Booties, 3½"h, $3.00-4.00; Stork
w/Square Planter, 8"h, $3.00-4.00;
#648, Pair Booties on sq. base, 4½"h,
$3.00-4.00. (Front Row): #B-3107,
Lamb Planter, 5"h, $3.00-4.00; Boy
w/arms up, 6"h, $3.00-4.00; #3568,
"Tuffy" Boxer, 5"l, $3.00-4.00; Baby
w/guitar, 6½"l, $3.00-4.00.

Photo 104. #3088, Swans, pr., 7½"h,
$6.00-8.00 ea. #3422, Window Planter,
18"l, $5.00-6.00.

Photo 105. Haeger 78-1, Kitten Container, 5"h, $3.00-4.00. #R-1657, Cooky Barrel, 12½"h, $20.00-25.00. Haeger 78-2, A-B-C Container, 5"h, $3.00-4.00.

Photo 106. #R-1500, Modern Double Loop Vase, 8"h, $8.00-10.00. #R-1627, Fish Wall Pocket (or Hanging Planter), 13"l, $6.00-8.00. #3306, Horsehead Vase, (also referred as bookends) 9"h, $6.00-8.00 ea.

Photo 107. #R-1265, Colt Figurine, "h, $10.00-12.00. #R-1598, Bullfighter Ashtray, raised design, black bottom, 0"w, $10.00-12.00. Haeger USA, "McDonough Power Cooperative" advertising ashtray, 5½"w, $3.00-4.00. Haeger USA, "Say It With Flowers" advertising ashtray, 5¼"w, $3.00-4.00.

Photo 108. (Sesquicentennial Ashtrays-1818/1968): #R-1892-S, "Land of Lincoln" Ashtray, 12"l, $6.00-8.00. #R-1098, "Jane Addams" Ashtray, 7"l, $4.00-6.00. #R-1096, "Stephen A. Douglas" Ashtray, 7"l, $4.00-6.00. #R-1095, "Lincoln" Ashtray, 7"l, $4.00-6.00. #R-182L, Swan, 8"h, $10.00-12.00.

Photo 109. "Spirit of '76 - Randall Creations for a Beautiful America" advertising ashtray, $4.00-5.00. Haeger-1973, Vase with bottom lettering: "Chapter K Macomb, Illinois" (accompanied by a star), $3.00-4.00.

Photo 110. #3212, Double Cornucopia on sq. base, 16"l, $6.00-8.00.

Photo 111. "Royal Haeger", Country Classic Coffee Mugs, 4½"h, $2.00-3.00 ea. #854-H, Fish Platter, stoneware, 18"l, $6.00-8.00.

Photo 112. #R-421, Console Bowl, 14″l, $20.00-25.00. #R-473, Twinstalk Candleholders, 10″h, $12.00-15.00 ea.

Photo 113. #R-472, Russian Lady, 12″h, $30.00-35.00.

Photo 114. #R-917, Peter Pan Vase, 10″h, $18.00-20.00.

Photo 115. #R-414, Swan, head down, 10"h, $22.00-25.00. #R-496, Bud Vase, 8"h, $5.00-8.00.

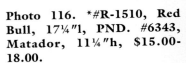

Photo 116. *#R-1510, Red Bull, 17¼"l, PND. #6343, Matador, 11¼"h, $15.00-18.00.

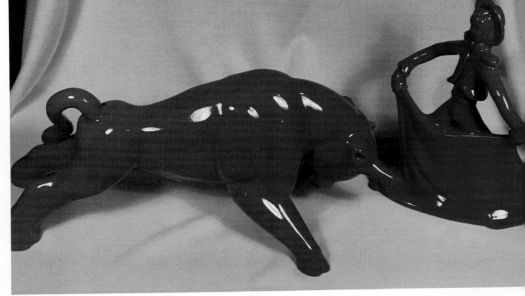

Photo 117. #R-475, Calla Lily Bookends, 6"h, $15.00-20.00 pr. #R-712, Bird of Paradise, small, 9¼"h, $15.00-18.00.

Photo 119. #R-1375, Green Wicker Basket, 9"h, $8.00-10.00.

Photo 118. #R-856, Tall Swan, 13"h, $15.00-20.00.

Photo 120. #990, Madonna, large, 13", $20.00-25.00. #374, Madonna, small, 6", $4.00-6.00.

Photo 121. #R-319, Wolfhound (head-up), 7″h, $22.00-25.00.

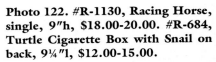

Photo 122. #R-1130, Racing Horse, single, 9″h, $18.00-20.00. #R-684, Turtle Cigarette Box with Snail on back, 9¼″l, $12.00-15.00.

Photo 123. #855, Stork on Foliage (old), 9¼″h, $8.00-10.00. #R-664, 2-pc. dish with polar bear on lid (boko finish), 7½″w, $18.00-20.00.

Photo 124. #6202, Greyhound TV lamp/planter, 13"l, $20.00-25.00 complete.

Photo 125. #R-456, Wrap-Around Vase, 14"h, $15.00-20.00.

Photo 127. #5228, Crepe Ginger Table Lamp, 23¾"h, $30.00-35.00. #5349, Acanthus Leaf Table Lamp, 28"h, $30.00-35.00.

Photo 126. #6065, Modern Oblong Table Lamp, 27"h, $15.00-20.00. #3386, Gazelle Vase, 9"h, $6.00-8.00.

Photo G/B 1. #R-223. 3-Lily dish, 6″ dia., $8.00-10.00. #R-431, Calla Lily Candy Box, 7½″ dia. $8.00-10.00.

Photo G/B 2. #R-295, Plume Candleholders, 4″h, $4.00-6.00 ea. #R-523, Fan Vase, $15.00-18.00.

Photo G/B 3. #R-426, Cornucopia Vase w/nude, 8″h, $15.00-18.00. #R-358, Footed Bowl, 17″l, $10.00-12.00.

Photo G/B 4. #RG-150, 2-Handled Urn, black cascade, $5.00-8.00. #R-402, Pr. Black Dappled Horses, 5½″h, $8.00-10.00 ea.

Photo G/B 5. #R-131, Pr. Basket Vases w/fruit, $18.00-20.00 ea. #R-455, Bow Vase, 14″h, $15.00-20.00.

Photo G/B 6. #R-332A, Pr. Cornucopia Vases (straight), 8″h, $10.00-12.00 ea.

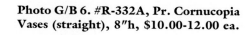

Photo G/B 7. #R-312, Pr. Cornucopia Candleholders, 4½″h, $4.00-6.00 ea. #R-246, Double Cornucopia Vase, 8″h, $20.00-25.00.

Photo G/B 8. #R-186, Pr. Large Bird of Paradise, 12¾"h, $20.00-25.00. #R-712, Small Bird of Paradise, $15.00-18.00.

Photo G/B 9. #R-1215, Ballet Vase, male; R-1215 Ballet Vase, female, 13½"h, $12.00-15.00 ea.

Photo G/B 10. #5038, Lamp - Gourd in Bowl Planter, $20.00-25.00.

Photo G/B 11. #5292, Lamp - Three Plumes with Bow, 26"h, $30.00-35.00. #5024, Lamp - Plume on Square Base, 19½"h, $30.00-35.00.

Photo G/B 12. #R-373, Bowl with fruit application, (3 different finishes), 20"l, $25.00-30.00.

Photo G/B 13. #R-546, Flower Candleholders, round and flat, $4.00-5.00 ea.

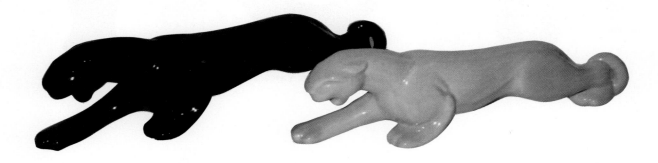

Photo G/B 14. #R-683, Panthers, 18"l, $15.00-20.00.

Photo G/B 15. #345S, Bowl, indents around and scalloped top, 5" dia., $8.00-10.00.

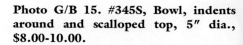

Photo G/B 16. #R-210 & 1006, Birds on Bowl, 7½″ dia., $10.00-12.00.

Photo G/B 17. #R-230, Cog Wheel Ashtray, 7½″ dia., $4.00-5.00.

Photo G/B 18. #R-886, Flat-sided Free Form Vase, $15.00-18.00. Matching vases, 10″h, $8.00-10.00 ea.

Photo G/B 19. #505, Mermaid, reclining, 21″l, $25.00-30.00.

Photo G/B 20. #R-790, Fighting Cock, head down, 11½"h, $20.00-22.00. #R-791, Fighting Cock, standing on tail, $20.00-22.00.

Photo G/B 21. #R-31, Peacock Gladiola Vase, 15"h, $40.00-45.00.

Photo G/B 22. #R-393, "Pegasus" Vase, 11½"H (75th Anniversary Sticker on cheek), $20.00-25.00.

Photo G/B 23. #5195, 2-Fawn Table Lamp, 24"h, $30.00-35.00.

Photo G/B 24. #R-1762, Haeger Red Realistic Rooster, PND.

Photo G/B 25. 5351, Flying Fish Table Lamp (w/original shade), 27"h, $40.00-45.00.

Photo G/B 26. #R-31, "Trio of Peacocks," (different positions and sizes) 15"h, $40.00-45.00. #R-453, 10"h, $12.00-15.00.

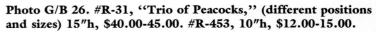

Haeger Then and Now

This photo entitled "Haeger Then and Now", depicts (from the late '30s) design R-248, Plume Console Vase, designer Royal A. Hickman - as Haeger *Then*. To the left of the Plume, depicting Haeger *Now*, is design #6034 Rendezvous, and to the right, design #6033 Lovers - designer C. Glenn Richardson.

The Future

"Although the company is over a century old, its outlook is not! Our 117 years of experience is yours from which to benefit. We are not looking back at the past century - only ahead to the next.

A company cannot survive without the support of its customers and friends, and we pause during this benchmark in our history to offer you our warmest thanks and appreciation. We pledge to each of you that we will do all that is possible to continue to lead, to innovate and to explore with just one goal in mind: to serve you much better with each passing year."

Additional Catalog Reprints

A focal point...

To lift *a room from the drab to the dramatic!*

Genuine
Haeger
Pottery

At better dealers everywhere

The HAEGER POTTERIES, Inc.
DUNDEE, ILLINOIS • MACOMB, ILLINOIS
WORLD'S LARGEST ART POTTERIES

Genuine
Haeger
Pottery

This lovely shell vase is typical of Royal Haeger Pottery — so graceful in design, and with such exquisite pastel coloring! No wonder women number their Royal Haeger pieces among their most cherished possessions.

Better dealers have Royal Haeger pottery in many lovely designs — be sure to see it but first buy your full quota of war bonds!

The HAEGER POTTERIES, Inc.
DUNDEE   ILLINOIS
WORLD'S LARGEST ART POTTER

Genuine
Haeger
Pottery

• **Decorative**
Distinctive
Different •

THE ARTISTIC DESIGN and fluid lines of Genuine Haeger Pottery will add distinction to any room; its colorful glaze will add warmth and beauty. After buying your next War Bond, see the unusual varieties of Genuine Haeger Pottery at better stores everywhere.

The HAEGER POTTERIES, Inc.
DUNDEE, ILL. • MACOMB, ILL.
WORLD'S LARGEST ART POTTERIES

Haeger Pottery

1943

ROYAL HAEGER

REGULAR HAEGER

(For description see following page)

R-313   R-282   R-314

WORLD'S LARGEST ART POTTERY   DUNDEE, ILINOIS

R-453, Small Peacock Vase, Height 10"
Available in Colors 2, 3, 7, 10, and 11

R-210, Bird Bowl, Width 7½"
R-220, Bird Candlestick, Height 3½"
Available in Colors 1 to 12

R-281, Sphere & Three Plumes, Height 10"
Available in Colors 2 and 3

R-437, 2½" x 5"   R-460, 5" x 12"   R-437
Console Set, Leaf Bowl and Leaf Candelholders
Bowl Available in Colors 2, 3, 4, 10, and 12   Candleholders Available in Colors 1 to 12

R-251, Onion Jug, Height 21"
Available in Colors 2, 3, and 7

R-309, Ruching Bowl, Length 12"
Available in Colors 2, 3, 4, 5, 10, and 12

R-430, Swan, Height 8"
Available in Colors 1 to 12

R-108, Vase, Height 7½"
Colors 1, 2, 3, 5, 7

R-182R, Small Swan Vase,
Height 8"
Available in Colors 1 to 12

R-182L, Small Swan Vase,
Height 8"
Available in Colors 1 to 12

R-301, Small Fan Vase, Height 9"
Available in Colors 1 to 12

R-358, Footed Bowl, Length 18", Width 8", Depth 3½"
Available in Colors 2, 3, 4, 5, 7, and 10

R-446, Height 14"
Colors 4, 6, 10 Only

R-387, Tall Modern Vase, Height 16"
Available in Colors 2, 3, 5, 7, 10, and 12

R-351, Shorter Modern Vase, 8½"
Available in Colors 2, 3, 4, 5, 7, and 12

R-445   R-436   R-445
Flower Pots, 3"x4½"—3½"x7¾"
Available in Manganese/Stain Only

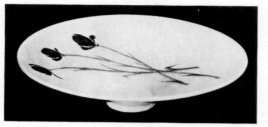

R-443, Coolie Hat Bowl, Diameter 16"
Available in Colors 2, 3, 5, and 7; also honey decorated

R-393. Horse Head Vase, Height 11½"   Available in Colors 4, 7, 10, and 11

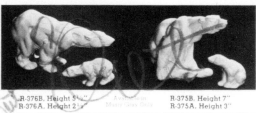

R-376B. Height 5½"   Available in   R-375B. Height 7"
R-376A. Height 2½"   Misty Gray Only   R-375A. Height 3"

R-408. Double Racing Horses. Height 10"
Available in Mellow Only

"CANNOT FURNISH"

R-132. Ram Bookends. 8"x9"

THE HAEGER POTTERIES, INC.   - 4 -   World's Largest Art Pottery

R-467. Goose Vase. Diameter 7"x16¼"

"CANNOT FURNISH"

R-424. Bucking Cowboy. Height 13"

R-451. Horse and Colt, Height 10", Length 13½"
Available in Amber Only

"CANNOT FURNISH"

R-402. Height 5"   R-400. Height 5"   R-401. Height 4"
Available in Misty Gray Color

R-415. Big Horse. Length 13"
Available in Manganese

R-284. Trout Flower Vase. Height 7"
Available in Colors 1 to 12

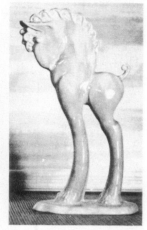

R-235. Colt Flower Holder,
Head Down. Height 12½"
Available in Colors 1 to 12

R-414. Swan. Width 12". Height 10"
Available in Colors 1 to 12

R-103. Small Horse.
Height 7"

R-203. Candle Holder
Height 5½"

THE HAEGER POTTERIES, INC. — 6 — World's Largest Art Pottery

R-115. Gazelle Vase. Height 13"
Available in Colors 1, 4, 5, and 7

R-373. Bowl. Length 19"
Available in Colors 2, 3, 5, 9, 10, and 12

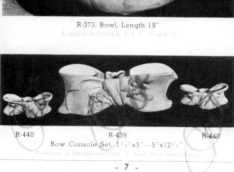

R-440   R-439   R-440
Bow Console Set. 1½"x5" — 5"x12½"
Available in Manganese Rose or Aqua Blue-Matte Gray

R-36. Swan. Height 16". Width 10"
Available in Colors 1, 2, 3, 4, 5, and 9

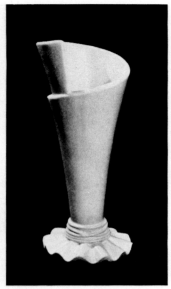

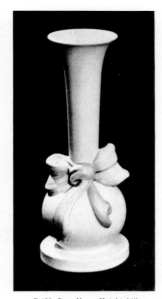

R-456, Wrap-Around Spiral, Height 14"
Available in Colors 4, 5, 7, and 12

R-454, Chinese Vase, Height 15"
Available in White Crystal and Honey Travertine.

R-455, Bow Vase, Height 14"
Available in Colors, Gloss White with Blue Bow; Green Agate with Green Bow; Mauve Agate with Mauve Bow

R-438, 1"x3½"   R-371, Length 13"   R-438
Console Set, Low Wave Bowl and Rosebud Candleholders
Bowl Available in Colors 1 to 12   Candleholders Available in Colors 1 to 12

R-450, Long Narrow Bowl, Length 23"
Available in Colors 2, 3, 4, and 7

THE HAEGER POTTERIES, INC.   - 8 -   World's Largest Art Pottery

R-297, Shell Bowl, Length 14", Width 8"
Available in Colors 2, 3, 5, 7, and 11

R-357, Bowl, 16"x7"
Available in Colors 1, 2, 3, 4, 6, and 10

R-228, Cornucopia Vase, Height 9"
Available in Colors 1 to 12
R-312, Candleholders, Height 5"
Available in Colors 1 to 12

R-246, Double Cornucopia Vase, Height 8", Length 15"
Available in Colors 1 to 12

R-299, Snail Shell Vase, Length 11", Height 7", Width 3¼"
Available in Colors 1 to 12

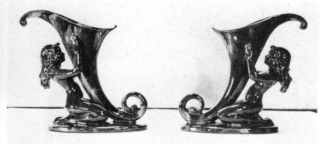

R-426, Cornucopia with Nude, Height 8"
Available in Colors 1 to 12

R-31, Peacock Vase, Height 15"
Available in Colors 2, 3, 7, 10, and 11

R-186, Bird of Paradise Vase, Height 12¾", Length 9", Width 4½"
Available in Colors 2, 3, 4, and 7

R-458, Small Triple Shell Candy Dish,
Length 6½"
Available in Colors 1 to 12

R-459, Large Triple Candy Dish,
Length 9"
Available in Colors 1 to 12

R-457, Triple Leaf Candy Dish,
Length 9½"
Available in Colors 1 to 12

R-279. Tall Basket, Height 21", Length 9", Width 9"   Available in Colors 1, 2, 3, 4, 7 and 11

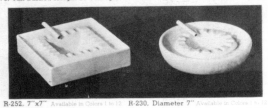

R-252. 7"x7" Available in Colors 1 to 12   R-230. Diameter 7" Available in Colors 1 to 12

R-335. Shell Bowl, Diameter 14", Depth 3½"
Available in Colors 2, 3, 4, 5 and 11

R-286. Leaf Plate, Length 12"
Available in Colors 3, 4, 5, 7, 11, and 12

THE HAEGER POTTERIES, INC.   - 12 -   World's Largest Art Pottery

---

R-285. Swan Vase, Height 9", Length 6", Width 4"
Available in Colors 1 to 12

R-475.
Book Ends.
Height 6"

Available in
Antbut Only

R-409. Pillow Vase, Height 11½"
Available in Mallow Only

R-397. Candleholder, Length 8"
Available in Colors 1 to 12

D-1001. Vase, Height 7½"
Available in Colors 1 to 12

R-323. Corrugated Vase,
Height 9"
Available in Colors 1 to 12

Dundee, Illinois   - 13 -   **THE HAEGER POTTERIES, INC.**

R-126A, Small Leaf Plate, 10"x11"
R-126, Large Leaf Plate, 16"x16"
Available in Colors 4, 5, 7, 11, and 12

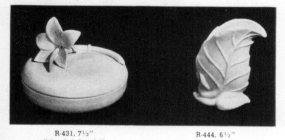

R-431, 7½"
Colors 2, 4, 8, and 10

R-444, 6½"
Colors 1 to 12

R-224, Low
Daisy Bowl,
Diameter 12"

Available in
Colors 1 to 12

R-208, Seagull Vase.
Height 16", Length 8", Width 3½"
Available in Colors 2, 3, 4, 6, and 7

R-287, Bird House,
Height 9½", Length 7½", Width 4¼"
Available in Colors 1 to 12

R-295, Height 4"   R-248, Height 10"   R-295
Console Set, Plume Candleholders
Available in Colors 1 to 12

R-320, Elm Leaf Vase, Height 12"
Available in Colors 2, 3, 4, 5, 7, 11 and 12

R-434, Hen Pheasant, 7"x15"—R-435, Rooster Pheasant, 11"x12"
Available in Colors 2, 3, 5, 8, and 11

R-432, 8½"x9"
Colors 2, 3, 5, 8, and 11

R-328, Oval Bowl Plume Feet, Height 8"
Available in Colors 1 to 12 with exception of 11

R-322, Shell Cornucopia, Length 7½"
Available in Colors 1 to 12

R-441, Height 11½"
Available in Colors 1 to 12

R-472, Vase, Height 12"
Available in Mauve Grey Only

THE HAEGER POTTERIES, INC.   — 16 —   World's Largest Art Pottery

R-452, Height 16"
Available in Colors 2, 3, 4, 5, 10, and 12

R-332A, Height 8"   R-332B, Height 11"
Tall Cornucopias
Available in Colors 1 to 12

R-290, Cut Out V Bowl, Diameter 10"
Available in Colors 1, 2, 3, and 7

R-448, Diameter 3½"   R-447, Diameter 4½"   R-449, Length 4½"
Small Shell   Large Shell   Leaf
Ash Trays, Available in Colors 1 to 12

R-278, Large Spiral Plume, Width 9"
R-277, Small Spiral Plume, Width 6"
Available in Colors 1 to 12

R-321, Shell Vase, Height 8", Width 5"
Available in Colors 1 to 12

R-138, Leaf Vase, Height 12¼", Length 12", Width 5½"
Available in Colors 1, 2, 3, 4, 9, 7, and 11

D-1028, Bee Hive Vase, Height 7½"
Available in Colors 1 to 12

ROYAL HAEGER POTTERIES ARE NOTED FOR THEIR ARTISTIC QUALITIES AND BEAUTY OF COLORINGS

R-360, Height 11½"   R-359, Width 11", Height 7½"
Available in Colors 1 to 12

R-140, Deep Fluted Oval Bowl, Length 18"
Available in Colors 1 to 12

R-364, Height 13"
Nude with Seal
Block
Available in Colors
1 to 12 with the
exception of 11

R-293, Violin Bowl, Length 16½"
Available in Colors 2, 3, 9, 10, and 11

R-433, Triple Candleholders, Length 11½"
Available in Colors 1 to 12

R-370, Dutch Cup Bowl, Length 19", Width 6½", Depth 4½"
Available in Colors 2, 3, 4, 7, 11 and 12

R-470, Fluted Bowl, 12"x2½"
Available in Colors 1 to 12

R-466, Bowl, 6"x15"
Available in Colors 1 to 12

R-372, Round Fluted Bowl, Width 13½"
Available in Colors 2, 3, 4, 5, 5, 10, 11, and 12
R-103, Small Horse, Height 7"
Available in Colors 1 to 12

R-418, 6"x9"   R-421, 7"x14"   R-418
Console Set Bowl Available in Colors 1 to 12 with exceptions 20, 11
Candleholders Available in Colors 1 to 12 with exceptions 20, 11

R-476, Bowl, 4½"x15"
Available in Colors 1 to 12

R-386, Basket, Length 12", Height 9", Width 2½"
Available in Colors 1 to 12 and

R-271, Sail Fish Vase, Height 9"
Available in Colors 1 to 12

R-33, Vase, Height 13"
Available in Colors 3, 4, 5, 9, and 11

R-303, Laurel Wreath Bow
Height 12"
Available in Colors 2, 3, 4, 6,
11 and 12

R-298, Cornucopia Shell Vase,
Length 11", Height 9", Width 5"
Available in Colors 2, 3, 4, 5, 6, and 11

R-442, Bowl, Length 18"
Available in Colors 1 to 12

R-473, Width 9", Height 10"
Available in Colors 1 to 12

R-363, Height 10"
Available in Colors 1 to 12

R-407, Height 6½"
Available in Colors 1 to 12

R-422, Vase, Height 6"
Available in Colors 1 to 12

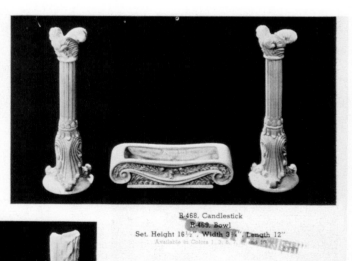

R-474, Vase, Height 9", Top 5"
Manganese Stain Only

R-468, Candlestick
R-469, Bowl
Set, Height 16½", Width 3¾", Length 12"
Available in Colors 1, 3, 6,

R-602
Height 5½"

R-604
Height 5½"

R-603
Height 5½"
Manganese Stain Only

R-601
Height 7"

R-600
Height 9"

R-318, Height 7"

R-319, Height 7"
Available in Colors 5, 6, and 8

"CANNOT FURNISH"

Regular Haeger Pottery

These beautiful Vases and Planters make pleasing, inexpensive gifts. Each of these is a proven fast-seller and could be stocked to round out your line.

"CANNOT FURNISH"

3259. Squirrel, Length 4"

614. Duck, Length 5"

3244. Vase, 4"

3246. Cornucopia Vase, 4"

3238. Vase, 4"

3252. Plume Vase, 4"

UPPER ROW
3240. Vase, 4"   3236. Vase, 4"   3243. Vase, 4"
LOWER ROW
3229. Bootie, 4"   3251. Squirrel, 3½"

3248. Bunny, 3¾"

THE HAEGER POTTERIES, INC.   - 24 -   World's Largest Art Pottery

June Jubilee ... Fragrant roses glamourously arranged in Royal Haeger Fluted Bowl with separate Bird Block. One of many colorful Haeger designs to brighten your home ... available at leading stores everywhere.

Haeger
POTTERIES INC.
DUNDEE, ILLINOIS

FLOWER FUN—Colorful new booklet pictures flower arrangements like that shown above, using readily available flowers. Send 10c (coin) to Dept. 106.

A Royal Haeger vase or bowl will vie with your choicest garden flowers for beauty of color and lovely design. Together they make an exquisite ensemble, breath-taking in sheer beauty.

If your war bond purchases permit, select a Royal Haeger vase in which to display your summer blooms. Most better dealers have Haeger Pottery.

The HAEGER POTTERIES, Inc.
DUNDEE, ILLINOIS
WORLD'S LARGEST ART POTTERY

Royal Haeger *Artware*

This supplement to your permanent catalog pictures and describes forty-one designs representing a broad review of current tastes and trends. Many of these designs were unanimously elected to the "Fabulous Fifty-One"*. Your attention is particularly directed to the sheer loveliness of the new Haeger colors, Cotton White and Woodland Brown, and to the new Foam overflow glaze.

Haeger
Royal 51

*Hundreds of lamp and artware designs were placed before a group of experienced merchandisers who screened them for those with most obvious retailing potential. One hundred and eighteen designs were thus voted into our line; fifty-one achieved *unanimous* approval. Each design in this group is considered one of the year's most notable art expressions.

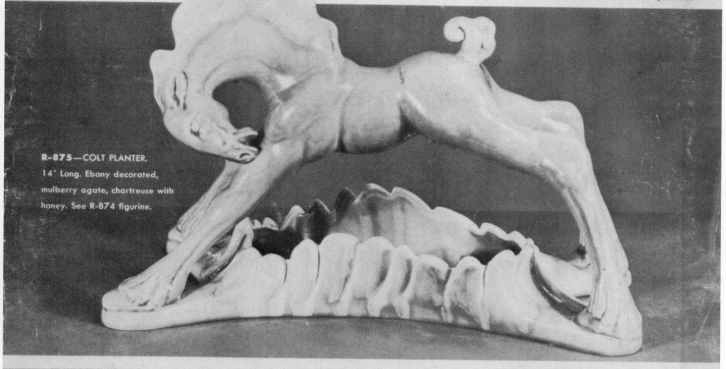

R-875—COLT PLANTER. 14" Long. Ebony decorated, mulberry agate, chartreuse with honey. See R-874 figurine.

R-896—SLEEPING CAT. 7" Long. Ebony, pearl grey.

R-880—RESTING STAG FIGURINE. 14½" Long. Oxblood, mulberry agate, ebony, pearl grey decorated, chartreuse with honey. See R-881 planter.

R-873—FREE FORM ASH BOWL. 8½" Long. Green agate with foam, ebony with foam, pink crackle, woodland brown with foam, chartreuse with foam.

R-860—TRIO ASHTRAY. 7½" Long. Chartreuse with foam, dark green with foam, ebony with foam, woodland brown with foam.

R-862—TRIANGLE ASHTRAY. 7" Long. Chartreuse with foam, dark green with foam, ebony with foam, woodland brown with foam.

R-898—SITTING CAT. 6" High. Ebony, pearl grey.

R-883—DOUBLE RACING HORSE. PLANTER. 11" High. Cotton white with chartreuse, chartreuse with green agate, silver spray with pearl grey, ebony with chartreuse. See R-882 figurine.

R-897—STANDING CAT. 7" High. Ebony, pearl grey.

THE HAEGER POTTERIES, INC.
DUNDEE, ILLINOIS

R-893—TULIP MODERN VASE. 12" High. Oxblood with white, green agate, woodland brown with white, chartreuse with honey, pearl grey decorated.

R-886—FLATSIDED FREE FORM VASE. 10" High. Green agate, pearl grey decorated, chartreuse with honey and dark green, woodland brown, ebony.

R-884—FREE FORM VASE. 18" High. Green agate, pearl grey decorated, chartreuse with honey and dark green, woodland brown, ebony.

The Finest IN CURRENT ABSTRACT, CLASSIC

R-885—FREE FORM VASE. 12" High. Green agate, pearl grey decorated, chartreuse with honey and dark green, woodland brown, ebony.

R-899—PALETTE VASE. 12½" High. Pearl grey decorated, green agate with chartreuse, woodland brown with white, chartreuse with green stain.

R-900—MODERN SCROLL VASE. 6" High. Green agate, ebony, chartreuse with honey, pearl grey decorated, slate blue.

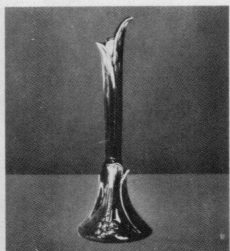

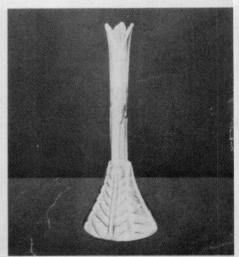

R-895—MODERN VASE. 11" High. Green agate with chartreuse, woodland brown with white and chartreuse, pearl grey decorated and silver spray, chartreuse with green stain.

R-891—CONVENTIONAL BUD VASE. 12" High. Green agate, chartreuse with honey, mulberry, agate, yellowdrip.

R-892—MODERN BUD VASE. 12" High. green agate, chartreuse with honey, mulberry agate, yellowdrip.

R-903—FLYING DUCK VASE. 9" High. Green agate with white, mulberry agate with white, plum decorated, slate blue.

R-904 — SETTING DUCK VASE. 9" High. Green agate with white, mulberry agate with white, plum decorated, slate blue.

ND WHIMSICAL DESIGN
identified by this Trademark...

Haeger Royal 51

R-878—OYSTER SHELL. 9" High. Green agate, pearl grey decorated, chartreuse with honey, woodland brown with white.

R-902—FEATHER FAN VASE. 6" High. Green agate, oxblood with honey, chartreuse with honey, mulberry agate, plum decorated, slate blue.

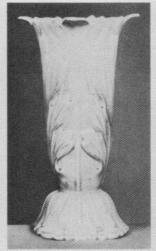

R-905—RENAISSANCE VASE. 16" High. Chartreuse with yellow, woodland brown with white and chartreuse, mulberry agate, green agate.

R-888—GOOSE QUILLS VASE. 17¼" High. Oxblood with honey and white, green agate, chartreuse with honey, mulberry agate, plum decorated.

R-879—FLATSIDED ACANTHUS LEAF VASE. 11" High. Woodland brown with white and chartreuse, green agate, mulberry agate, chartreuse with yellow.

R-917—PETER PAN VASE. 10" High. Chartreuse, slate blue, pearl grey decorated, green agate.

R-887—SHELL VASE. 13" High. Green agate, pearl grey decorated, chartreuse with honey and yellow.

R-901—SWORDFISH. 6" High. Green agate, chartreuse with honey, tortoise brown.

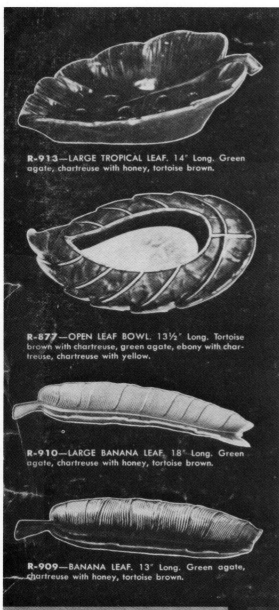

R-913—LARGE TROPICAL LEAF. 14" Long. Green agate, chartreuse with honey, tortoise brown.

R-877—OPEN LEAF BOWL. 13½" Long. Tortoise brown with chartreuse, green agate, ebony with chartreuse, chartreuse with yellow.

R-910—LARGE BANANA LEAF. 18" Long. Green agate, chartreuse with honey, tortoise brown.

R-909—BANANA LEAF. 13" Long. Green agate, chartreuse with honey, tortoise brown.

Haeger COLOR MAKES EACH DESIGN GLOW WITH LIFE

R-894—LOW FLATSIDED BOWL. 18" Long. Green agate, pearl grey decorated, yellowdrip.

R-915—LARGE ELEPHANT EAR LEAF. 13" Long. Green agate, chartreuse with honey, tortoise brown.

R-911—WINE LEAF. 10" Long. Green agate, chartreuse with honey, tortoise brown.

R-907—LILY LEAF. 8" Wide. Green agate, chartreuse with honey, tortoise brown.

R-914—SMALL TROPICAL LEAF. 10" Long. Green agate, chartreuse with honey, tortoise brown.

R-908—LARGE LILY LEAF. 11" Wide. Green agate, chartreuse with honey, tortoise brown.

R-912—LARGE WINE LEAF. 15" Long. Green agate, chartreuse with honey, tortoise brown.

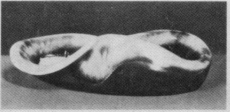

R-876—FREE FORM FIGURE EIGHT BOWL. 14" Long. Green agate with foam, ebony with foam, pink crackle, woodland brown with foam, chartreuse with foam.

R-916—SMALL ELEPHANT EAR LEAF. 11" Long. Green agate, chartreuse with honey, tortoise brown.

LITHO IN U.S.

Selections from the line
of
ROYAL HAEGER
Ceramic Artwares
for
1952

ROYAL Haeger POTTERY

The Haeger Potteries, INC.
DUNDEE, ILL. MACOMB, ILL.

A PARTIAL SELECTION OF DESIGNS FROM THE EXTENSIVE NEW 1952 LINE

ROYAL Haeger POTTERY

All designs are Styled by Jury

Each Haeger design, after it is developed in sketch form by the Art Staff, must receive the approval of a qualified Jury before the design can become a part of the Haeger line.

The Jury consists of individual merchandisers and consumers from every section of the country who reflect style demands of their areas.

"Style by Jury" is your assurance that each catalogue design has been critically evaluated as to its popular appeal and has been selected by a majority of the Jury, not only for its beauty but for the profit-making sales potential it represents to you.

CONSOLE SETS POPULARLY

R-1133—RECTANGULAR BOWL Gr. agate, char., oxblood, ebony. 17" long. $6. R-1134—ASHTRAY CANDLEHOLDER Some colors. 6½" long. $2.50.

R-1175—WAVE CANDLEHOLDERS Green agate, chartreuse, oxblood, walnut. 5" long. Retail price $4. pr. R-1176—BOWL WITH WAVES Same colors. 16" long. Retail price $7.

R-967—STAR FISH BOWL Char./honey, green agate, pearl grey dec., gun metal. 14" wide. $5. R-968—STAR FISH CANDLEHOLDERS Same colors. 6" wide. $3. pr.

R-224—DAISY BOWL Sil. sp/char., char./honey, gr. ag. 12". $6. R-363—NUDE ASTRIDE FISH BLOCK Sil. sp., char., gr. ag., gr. crystal. 10" high. $4.

R-641—STALLION BOOKEND PLANTER Oxblood/white, ebony, chartreuse, green agate, cotton white. 8½" high. Retail price $6. pr.

R-755—MODERN FORM BOWL Dk. gr/char., ebony/char., woodland br./turquoise. 14" long. $5. R-756—CANDLEHOLDERS Dk. gr., ebony, woodland br., 5½" long. $3. pr.

R-689—SQUARE SHALLOW BOWL Green crystal, green agate, ebony. 10½" long. $5. R-690—SQUARE CHINESE CANDLEHOLDERS Some colors. 5" long. $4. pr.

R-484—GARDEN BOWL Ebony/char., sil. sp./char., gr. ag. 14" long. $4. R-485—UPRIGHT CANDLEHOLDERS Char., ebony, sil. sp., gr. ag. 7½" long. $4. pr.

R-313—TIGRESS FIGURINE Ebony, amber. 12" long. $10. R-282—OBLONG BOWL Ebony, amber. 8" long. $9.50. R-314—TIGER FIG. Ebony, amber. 11" long. $10.

2

ALL PRICES SUBJECT TO CUSTOMARY DISCOUNT.

STYLED and PRICED

R-495—LARGE PANTHER FIGURINE Ebony, cotton white, 24" long. Retail price $10.

R-657—GONDOLIER PLANTER Available in chartreuse, ebony or green agate with separate planter pots. 18" long. Retail price $12.

R-948—FLARED BOWL Gr. ag./char./honey, char./yel., ebony, pearl grey/sil. sp. 15" long. $6. R-949—FLARED CANDLE-HOLDERS gr. ag., pearl grey dec., char./honey, ebony. 3¼" high. $3. pr.

R-989—WINGED BOWL Green agate, chartreuse/honey, oxblood/honey, pearl grey dec. 12" long. Retail price $3.

R-371—WHIRLING BOWL Gr. ag., char./honey, mul. ag. sp. 13" long. $4. R-438—ROSEBUD CANDLE HOLDERS gr. ag., char., ebony, mul. ag., sil. sp., gr. crystal. 4" wide. $2.50 pr.

R-953—LOW DRAPED BOWL Gr. ag., char./honey, oxblood/wt., pearl grey, yellowdrip. 17" long. $6. R-954—DRAPED CANDLEHOLDERS Same colors. 3½" high. $3; pr.

R-312—CORNUCOPIA CANDLEHOLDERS Woodland br., mul., gr. ag., sil. sp., char., ebony, pearl grey, cot. wt., walnut, gr. crystal. 5" high. $3. pr. R-476—BEADED BOWL Gr. ag., ebony/chartreuse, sil. sp./char. 15" long. $5.70.

R-985—OYSTER SHELL BOWL Green agate, chartreuse, ebony, mulberry agate, pearl grey 16" wide. Retail price $9.50.

R-309—RUCHING BOWL Gr. ag., char./yel., ebony/char., sil. sp./char. 14½" wide. $6. R-360—TROPICAL FISH BLOCK Gr. ag., char., mul. ag., pearl grey, sil. sp. 11" high. $4.

R-456—9" FISH GLOBE STAND WITH MER-MAID Available in green agate, chartreuse and honey with removable fish globe. 11" high. Retail price $15.

THE HAEGER POTTERIES, INC., DUNDEE, ILL. MACOMB, ILL.

3

....VASES WITH

R-1138—OVAL WRAPAROUND BOWL Gr. agate, char., oxblood, woodland brown, yellow. 6" high. Retail price $4.

R-901—6" SWORD FISH VASE Green agate, chartreuse/honey, woodland brown. Retail price $2. R-902—6" FEATHER FAN VASE Gr. agate, char./honey, oxblood/honey, mulberry agate, walnut. Retail price $3.

R-1136—FISH VASE Gr. agate, char., oxblood, pearl grey, yellow-drip. 6½" high. Retail price $3.

R-1140—DOUBLE LEAF VASE Green agate, chartreuse, oxblood, yellowdrip walnut. 8" high. Retail price $2.50.

R-1141—ANGEL VASE Gr. agate, char., yellowdrip, cotton white. 7" high. Retail price $2.50.

R-651—PILLOW VASE Green agate, chartreuse/honey, mulberry agate, cotton white. 8" high. Retail price $2.50.

R-900—6" MODERN SCROLL VASE Green agate, ebony, chartreuse/honey, pearl grey dec. Retail price $2.

R-833—12" FLATSIDED VASE Chartreuse/honey, green agate, oxblood, honey, pearl grey. Retail price $5.

R-1139—WRAPAROUND VASE Green agate, chartreuse, oxblood, woodland brown, yellow. 7" high. Retail price $3.50.

R-723—FEATHER VASE Green agate, chartreuse, slate blue, walnut. 9½" high. Retail price $3.50.

R-301—FAN VASE Green agate, chartreuse/honey, walnut. 9" high. Retail price $2.50.

4

GORGEOUS NEW GLAZE

R-879—FLATSIDED ACAN-
THUS LEAF VASE Wood-
land br./char., gr. agate,
mulberry agate, char./yel.
11" high. Retail price $5.

R-886—10" FLATSIDED FREE
FORM VASE Gr. agate,
char./honey, pearl grey
dec., woodland br./ebony,
cot. wt. Retail price $6.

R-1158—LOW PILLOW VASE
Gr. agate, char., oxblood,
ebony, pearl grey. 6" high.
Retail price $3.

R-1159—VERTICAL PILLOW
VASE Gr. ag., char., oxblood,
ebony, pearl grey. 8" high. Retail price $3.

R-1142—SWIRL VASE Gr. agate,
char., ebony, yellowdrip, walnut. 12½" high. Retail price $4.

R-1124—VASE Gr. agate, chartreuse, woodland brown, slate
blue. 8" high. Retail price $3.

ALL PRICES SUBJECT TO CUSTOMARY DISCOUNT

R-856—TALL SWAN VASE
Green agate, cotton white.
13" high. Retail price $6.

R-857—GAZELLE HEAD VASE Gr. Agate, char./
honey, oxblood/honey, cotton white. 12" high.
Retail price $3.50.

R-264—TROUT VASE Green
agate, chartreuse, mulberry
agate. 7½" high. Retail
price $3.70.

R-271—SAILFISH VASE
Green agate, chartreuse,
mulberry agate, cotton
white. 9" high. Retail $3.70.

R-246—DOUBLE CORNUCOPIA
VASE Green agate, char./honey,
woodland brown/char., walnut. 8"
high. Retail price $11.

R-855—LEAF VASE Green
agate, chartreuse/honey. 11"
high. Retail price $3.

R-904—9" SETTING DUCK VASE Green
agate/white, mulberry agate/white, slate
blue. $3.50.

THE HAEGER POTTERIES, INC.,   DUNDEE, ILL. MACOMB, ILL.   5

VASES ARE

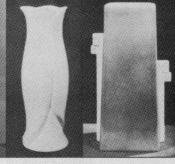

R-884—18" FREE FORM VASE
Gr. ag., char./honey, pearl
grey, woodland br., cotton
white. Retail price $10.

R-452—MORNING GLORY
VASE Green agate, char-
treuse, cotton white, walnut.
16" high. Retail price $9.

R-351—ONION JUG Green
agate, oxblood, slate blue,
yellow drip. 20½" high. Retail price $9.50.

R-693—WRAP AROUND VASE
Available in green agate,
char./honey. 18" high. Retail price $8.

R-691—SQUARE VASE Avail-
able in green agate, char./
honey, pearl grey. 7½"
high. Retail price $8.

R-1168—LARGE SAILFISH VASE Available in green
agate, chartreuse, green crystal. 14½" long. Retail price $10.

THE HAEGER POTTERIES, INC.,   DUNDEE, ILL. MACOMB, ILL.

R-182—SWAN VASES, l & r.
Green agate, pearl grey dec.,
silver spray. 7½" high. Retail
price $2.50 ea.

R-386—BASKET VASE Green
agate/chartreuse, chartreuse/
honey, walnut. 8½" high. Retail price $6.

R-1115—BOWL Green agate,
oxblood, ebony, woodland
br. 13" wide. Retail price $4.

R-320—ELM LEAF VASE Green
agate, char./honey, green crystal, mulberry agate. 12" high.
Retail price $6.

R-138—LEAF VASE Available in
green agate, mulberry agate.
12" high. Retail price $6.

R-960—10" BANANA LEAF VASE Gr. agate,
char./honey, woodland brown, yellowdrip,
walnut. Retail price $3. R-961—14" BA-
NANA LEAF VASE $5.

6

STYLED BY JURY

R-706—RUNNING DEER VASE Gr. ag.,
pearl grey dec., cotton white. 14" tall. $3.50.
R-707—STANDING DEER VASE $3.50.

R-36—LARGE SWAN VASE Available
in cotton white, green agate, char./
honey. 13½" high. Retail price $9.

R-186—BIRD OF PARADISE Available
in green agate, chartreuse/honey. 13"
high. Retail price $9.

R-31—PEACOCK Available in green
agate, chartreuse. 15" high. Retail
price $11.

ALL PRICES SUBJECT TO CUSTOMARY DISCOUNT.

R-426—NUDE WITH COR-
NUCOPIA VASE Silver
spray/chartreuse, char./
treuse/honey, green agate.
8" high. Retail price $3.70.

R-978—10" ABSTRACT VASE Gr. ag. char./
honey, pearl grey dec., cotton wt., ebony.
Retail price $3. R-979—8" ABSTRACT VASE
$2.50. R-980—6" ABSTRACT VASE $3.

R-453—SMALL PEACOCK
Available in green agate,
chartreuse/honey. 10" high.
Retail price $5.

R-883—RACING HORSE PLANTER
Cotton white/char., char./green
agate, silver spray/pearl grey,
ebony/char. 17" long. Retail $20.

R-1123—VASE Gr. ag.
char., woodland br.
slate blue. 7" high.
Retail price $2.50.

R-1120—VASE Gr. ag.,
char. woodland br.
slate blue. 5½" high.
Retail price $2.

R-1121—VASE Gr. ag.,
char., woodland br.,
slate blue. 5¼" high.
Retail price $2.

7

PLANTERS.

IMPORTANT TO YOU

Haeger is the world's largest producer of Ceramic Artware
as a result of two basic policies.

Every design produced is critically inspected after each production step and rejected unless it meets, in flawless beauty,
the most rigid quality standards.

All designs are first qualified as to popular appeal by a "Style
Jury" before being admitted to the line.

**ALL PRICES SUBJECT TO
CUSTOMARY DISCOUNT**

R-709—13" HORN OF
PLENTY Gr. ag./char./
yellow, woodland br./
char., ebony/char., cot.
wt. $4.50.

R-466—CURVING BOWL Gr. agate, ebony/char.,
mulberry agate, gr. crystal, cotton white. 14½"
long. Retail price $3.50.

R-358—FOOTED BOWL Green agate, chartreuse/
honey, pearl grey. 17" long. Retail price $10.

R-816—PETAL BOWL Pearl grey
dec., char./honey, gr. agate.
10" long. Retail price $6.

R-534—HORN OF PLENTY VASE Available in green agate, chartreuse/yel-
low, walnut. 18" long. Retail price $12.

R-421—BOWL WITH CLUSTERS Green
agate, char./honey, oxblood. 14"
wide. Retail price $10.

R-770—FLARED BOWL Char./yel., gr.
ag./char., silver spray/char., woodland br./turq. 13" wide. Retail price
$6.

R-909—BANANA LEAF Green agate,
chartreuse/honey, woodland brown.
13" long. Retail price $3.

R-910—LARGE BANANA LEAF Available in green agate, char-
treuse/honey, woodland brown. 18" long. $5.

R-974—"S" SHAPED CANDLE BOWL
Ebony/char., pearl grey/silver spray,
dk. gr./char. 22½" long. Retail $8.

8

LEAVES and BOWLS

R-894—18" LOW FLATSIDED BOWL Available in green agate, pearl grey dec., yellowdrip. Retail price $10.

R-821—LARGE OVAL LEAF BOWL Available in green agate/chartreuse, ebony. 19" long. Retail price $12.

R-852—TRIPLE BALL PLANTER Green agate, pearl grey, yellowdrip, woodland brown. 11" long. Retail price $3.50.

R-540—TURTLE PLANTER Green crystal, green agate, mulberry agate, woodland brown. 14" long. Retail price $6.50.

R-1126—RECT. CONCAVE BOWL Oxblood, ebony, gr. crystal, dark green. 10½" long. Retail price $5.

R-916—SMALL ELEPHANT EAR LEAF Green agate, chartreuse/honey, woodland brown. 11" long. Retail price $3.70.

R-915—LARGE ELEPHANT EAR LEAF Green agate, chartreuse/honey, woodland brown. 13" long. Retail price $6.

R-893—12" TULIP MODERN VASE Oxblood/white, gr. agate, woodland brown/wt., char./honey, cotton white. Retail price $5.

R-834—11" TURTLE PLANTER Mulberry agate, green agate, green crystal, woodland brown. Retail price $5.

R-667—PLAIN 8½" BOWL Available in green agate only. Retail price $5.

R-370—DUTCH BOWL Green agate, chartreuse/honey, mul. agate, pearl grey dec. 18" long. Retail price $7.

R-126X—LARGE LEAF PLATE WITH DIVISIONS Available in green agate, chartreuse, walnut. 15½" wide. Retail price $9.50.

THE HAEGER POTTERIES, INC.,   DUNDEE, ILL. MACOMB, ILL.   9

SELECTED PLANTERS

R-812—GONDOLA Chartreuse, ebony, dark gr. 15½" long. Retail price $4.

R-1161—WINDOW BOX Gr. agate, char., ebony, pearl grey, woodland br. 13½" long. Retail price $6.

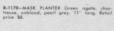
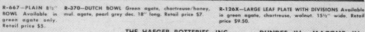

R-1170—MASK PLANTER Green agate, chartreuse, oxblood, pearl grey. 11" long. Retail price $6.

R-1146—STAG BOWL Green agate, chartreuse, pearl grey, woodland brown. 5¼" high. Retail price $5.50.

THE HAEGER POTTERIES, INC.,   DUNDEE, ILL. MACOMB, ILL.

R-881—RESTING STAG PLANTER Mulberry agate, ebony, pearl grey dec., char./honey, cotton white. 15" long. Retail price $12.

R-663—SQUARE CUBE PLANTER POT Green agate, chartreuse, pearl grey. 6¼" dia. Retail price $5.

R-754—DONKEY PLANTER Available in green agate, chartreuse, mulberry. 11" long. Retail price $3.

R-875—COLT PLANTER Ebony dec., chartreuse, cotton white. 14½" long. Retail price $15. R-874—FIGURINE Same colors. 14½" long. $9.50.

R-869—GAZELLE PLANTER Available in green agate, ebony dec., cot. wt. 13" high. Retail price $15.

R-563—ELEPHANT PLANTER Available in chartreuse/honey, ebony dec., walnut. 10½" high. Retail price $16.

10

NEW MODERN DESIGNS

R-1148—ROUND CUP ASH BOWL Green agate, chartreuse, oxblood, pearl grey. 6" wide. Retail price $2.50.

R-1149—DOVE ABSTRACT BOWL Green agate, chartreuse, oxblood, pearl grey. 8¼" long. Retail price $2.50.

R-1150—ABSTRACT SLICE BOWL Green agate, chartreuse, oxblood, pearl grey. 8½" long. Retail price $2.50.

R-1152—GOLF CLUB ASH TRAY Green agate, chartreuse, oxblood, pearl grey. 5" long. Retail price $2.

R-1155—8¼" ABSTRACT BIRD ASH BOWL Gr. agate, char., oxblood, pearl grey. Retail price $2.50.

R-1154—17" ABSTRACT BOWL Gr. agate, chartreuse, oxblood, pearl grey. Retail price $4.

ALL PRICES SUBJECT TO CUSTOMARY DISCOUNT

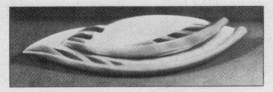

R-1151—10" ABSTRACT ANIMAL BOWL Gr. agate, char., oxblood, pearl grey. Retail price $3.

R-1156—DOUBLE PALM LEAF ASH TRAY Available in Green agate, chartreuse, pearl grey. 18½" long. Retail price $3.

ALL PRICES SUBJECT TO CUSTOMARY DISCOUNT

11

SMOKING ACCESSORIES

R-1145—CIGARETTE BOX Char., ebony, pearl grey, dk. green. 7½" long. Retail price $4.

ROYAL Haeger POTTERY

THE HAEGER POTTERIES, INC., DUNDEE, ILL. MACOMB, ILL.

ALL PRICES SUBJECT TO CUSTOMARY DISCOUNT

R-811—PALETTE ASHTRAY Available in Chartreuse, ebony, dark green. 9½" long. Retail price $1.50.

R-1172—ASHTRAY Char., ebony, pearl grey, dk. green. 6½" long. Retail price $2.

R-686—HORSEHEAD ASHTRAY Ebony, green agate, chartreuse, oxblood, cotton white. 6" wide. Retail price $2.80.

R-863—OPEN CIGARETTE BOX Ebony, dark green. 3½" high. Retail price $1.50.

R-864—ASHTRAY Same colors as R-863. 7" long. Retail price $2.

R-1129—ANGEL FISH ASH TRAY Green agate, chartreuse, ebony. Retail price $2.70.

R-230—COG WHEEL ASHTRAY Available in green agate, char., ebony, mulberry agate. 7½" dia. Retail price $3.

R-541—TURTLE ASH TRAY Green crystal, green agate, mulberry agate, woodland brown. 7½" long. Retail price $1.70.

R-685—HORSEHEAD CIGARETTE BOX Green agate, chartreuse, oxblood, ebony, cotton white. 7" long. $4.

R-860—TRIO ASH TRAY Chartreuse/foam, dark green/foam, ebony/foam, woodland br. foam. 7½" dia. Retail price $2.

R-873—FREE FORM ASH BOWL Green agate/foam, ebony/foam, woodland/foam. 8½" wide. Retail $4.

R-252—SQUARE ASH TRAY Ebony, chartreuse, green agate, mulberry agate. 7½" wide. Retail price $3.

12

—178—

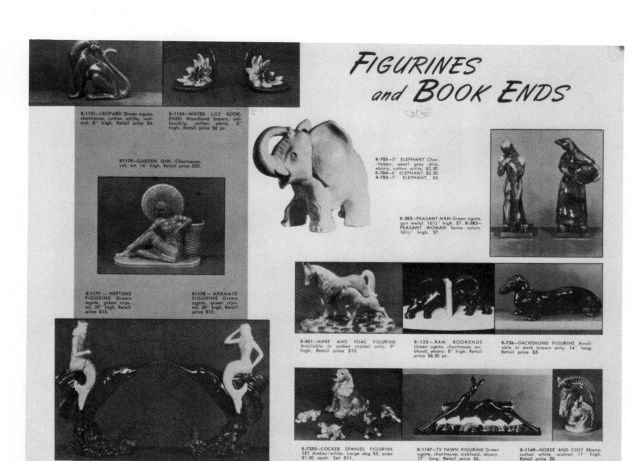

FIGURINES and BOOK ENDS

R-1131—LEOPARD Green agate, chartreuse, cotton white, walnut. 8" high. Retail price $4.

R-1146—WATER LILY BOOK ENDS Woodland brown, yellowdrip, cotton white. 3" high. Retail price $6 pr.

R1179—GARDEN GIRL Chartreuse, cot. wt. 14" high. Retail price $20.

R-785—5" ELEPHANT Char. /honey, pearl grey drip, ebony, cotton white. $2.50. R-784—6" ELEPHANT, $3.50. R-783—7" ELEPHANT, $5.

R-383—PEASANT MAN Green agate, gun metal. 16½" high. $7. R-383—PEASANT WOMAN Same colors. 16½" high. $7.

R-1177 — NEPTUNE FIGURINE Green agate, green crystal. 20" high. Retail price $15.

R-1178 — MERMAID FIGURINE Green agate, green crystal. 20" high. Retail price $15.

R-451—MARE AND FOAL FIGURINE Available in amber crystal only. 9" high. Retail price $13.

R-132—RAM BOOKENDS Green agate, chartreuse, oxblood, ebony. 8" high. Retail price $6.50 pr.

R-736—DACHSHUND FIGURINE Available in dark brown only. 14" long. Retail price $5.

R-7355—COCKER SPANIEL FIGURINE SET Amber/white. Large dog $5, pups $1.50 each. Set $11.

R-1147—TV FAWN FIGURINE Green agate, chartreuse, oxblood, ebony. 17" long. Retail price $6.

R-1169—HORSE AND COLT Ebony, cotton white, walnut. 11" high. Retail price $8.

13

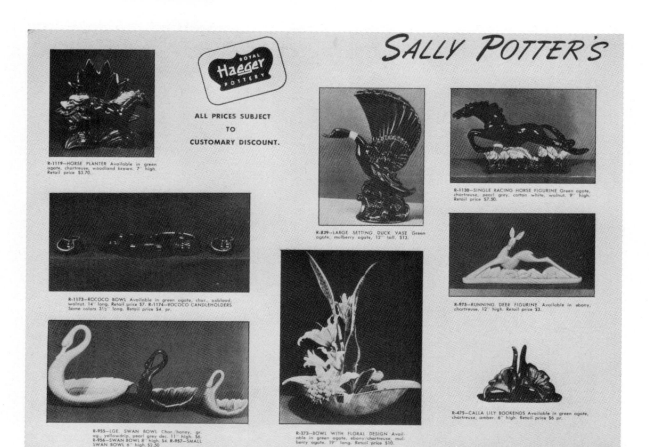

SALLY POTTER'S

ROYAL Haeger POTTERY

ALL PRICES SUBJECT TO CUSTOMARY DISCOUNT.

R-1119—HORSE PLANTER Available in green agate, chartreuse, woodland brown. 7" high. Retail price $3.70.

R-839—LARGE SETTING DUCK VASE Green agate, mulberry agate. 12" tall. $13.

R-1130—SINGLE RACING HORSE FIGURINE Green agate, chartreuse, pearl grey, cotton white, walnut. 9" high. Retail price $7.50.

R-1173—ROCOCO BOWL Available in green agate, char., oxblood, walnut. 14" long. Retail price $7. R-1174—ROCOCO CANDLEHOLDERS Same colors 3½" long. Retail price $4. pr.

R-975—RUNNING DEER FIGURINE Available in ebony, chartreuse. 12" high. Retail price $3.

R-955—LGE SWAN BOWL Char./honey, gr. ug., yellowdrip, pearl grey dec. 11" high. $6. R-956—SWAN BOWL 8" high. $4. R-957—SMALL SWAN BOWL 6" high. $2.50.

R-373—BOWL WITH FLORAL DESIGN Available in green agate, ebony/chartreuse, mulberry agate. 19" long. Retail price $10.

R-475—CALLA LILY BOOKENDS Available in green agate, chartreuse, amber. 6" high. Retail price $6 pr.

14

SELECTION OF ACCESSORIES

THE HAEGER POTTERIES, INC.,   DUNDEE, ILL. MACOMB, ILL.

R-1127—CANDLEHOLDERS Chartreuse, oxblood, ebony, green crystal, dark green. 4" long. Retail price $2.50 pr.

R-437—LEAF CANDLEHOLDERS Gr. ag., char., ebony, mulberry ag., pearl grey, woodland br., gr. crystal, sil. spray. 5" wide. Retail price $3 pr.

R-959—SWAN CANDLEHOLDER Green agate, chartreuse, pearl grey, yellowdrip. 5¼" high. Retail price $4. pr.

R-418—DOUBLE CANDLEHOLDER Green agate, char., oxblood, ebony, mulberry agate, pearl grey, 5½" high. Retail price $6. pr.

R-473—TWIN STALK CANDLEHOLDERS Green agate, chartreuse, oxblood, 11" high. Retail price $11.50 pr.

R-1162—STEPPED WALL POCKET Gr. ag., char., oxblood, pearl grey, yellowdrip. 4¼" wide. Retail price $2.50.

R-1163—WAVED WALL POCKET Gr. ag., char., oxblood, pearl grey, yellowdrip. 4" wide. Retail price $2.50.

R-1166—MODERN CANDY BOX Green agate, chartreuse, ebony, pearl grey. 10¼" long. Retail price $5.

R-725 — RECTANGULAR WALL POCKET Chartreuse, dark green, yellowdrip. 5" tall. Retail price $1.50.

R-1135—FLOWER WALL POCKET Chartreuse, oxblood, pearl grey, yellowdrip, walnut. 7" wide. Retail price $3.

15

The Haeger Potteries, Inc., The World's Largest Art Pottery — Dundee, Illinois

R1229 HARLEQUIN PLANTER. Green Agate, Coral, Chartreuse, Cotton White 12½" long Retail Price $10.00

R1230 DANCER PLANTER. Green Agate, Coral, Chartreuse, Cotton White 10½" tall. Retail Price $7.00

R1236 BIRD BOWL. Green Agate, Coral, Chartreuse, Walnut 14" long. Retail Price $8.00

R1224 GYPSY GIRL. Green Agate, Coral, Walnut, Chartreuse 16½" tall. Retail Price $15.00

R1225 GIRL WITH TWO BOWLS. Green Agate, Pearl Grey, Coral, Walnut 13" long Retail Price $7.00

R1226 HORSE PLANTER Chartreuse, Silver Spray, Dark Green, Walnut 8½" long Retail Price $5.00

R1184 HEART SHAPED ASHTRAY. Green Agate, Ebony, Coral, Chartreuse, Pearl Grey, Walnut 7½" long. Retail Price $5.00

R1196 EGG SHAPED DIVIDED BOWL. Green Agate, Chartreuse, Pearl Grey, Coral 12" long Retail Price $3.50

R1227 ELEPHANT PLANTER. Chartreuse, Pearl Grey, Walnut 8¼" high Retail Price $9.00

R1192 RECTANGULAR ASHTRAY Oxblood, Ebony, Dark Green, Walnut 6½" long Retail Price $12.00 doz.

R1204 SINGLE LEAF BOWL. Green Agate, Chartreuse, Pearl Grey, Coral 9" long. Retail Price $4.00

R277 FEATHER DISH. Ebony, Coral, Dark Green, Walnut 7" long Retail Price $2.00

R1198 COMEDY WALL MASK. Chartreuse, Oxblood, Ebony, Dark Green 11" high Retail Price $4.00

R1199 TRAGEDY WALL MASK. Chartreuse, Oxblood, Ebony, Dark Green 11" high Retail Price $4.00

THE HAEGER POTTERIES, INC., THE WORLD'S LARGEST ART POTTERY – DUNDEE, ILLINOIS

R1189 9" PINE CONE VASE. Green Agate, Pearl Grey, Coral, Walnut 9" high   Retail Price $4.00

R1190 12" PINE CONE VASE. Green Agate, Pearl Grey, Coral, Walnut 12" high   Retail Price $5.00

R1222 SMALL CLASSIC VASE. Green Agate, Chartreuse, Pearl Grey, Coral 13½" tall   Retail Price $5.00

R1223 LARGE CLASSIC VASE. Green Agate, Chartreuse, Pearl Grey, Coral 18" tall   Retail Price $8.00

R1210 CORNUCOPIA NUDE (R & L) Green Agate, Chartreuse, Coral, Silver Spray 7 3/4" high   Retail Price $3.50

R1221 BUTTERFLY VASE Green Agate, Coral, Chartreuse 7½" high Retail Price $4.00

R298 CONCH SHELL VASE Green Agate, Coral, Cotton White, Walnut 9" high Retail Price $5.00 - 1952

R1211 LEAF VASE. Green Agate, Coral, Chartreuse, Walnut 7½" high Retail Price $2.50

R1235 CLASSIC BUD VASE. Green Agate, Chartreuse, Oxblood, Pearl Grey 7¾" high Retail Price $3.00

R1191 SAIL FISH PLANTER BOWL Green Agate, Chartreuse, Oxblood, Walnut 11" long.   Retail Price $4.50

R1231 ST. FRANCIS FIGURINE - R1232 ST. FRANCIS BOWL.   Green Agate, Chartreuse Pearl Grey, Coral Figurine: 10½" high. Retail Price $2.00 - Bowl: 14" long. Retail Price $4.00

R1206 APPLE CANDLEHOLDERS R1205 APPLE BOWL. Green Agate, Chartreuse, Mulberry, Coral Candleholders: 2¼" high. Retail Price $3.50 Pr. Bowl: 15¼" long. Retail Price $7.50

R1218 SWAN FLOWER BOWL. Green Agate, Chartreuse, Coral, Walnut 11" long. Retail Price $4.50

R1197 TREBLE CANDLEHOLDERS - R1203 TWISTED SHELL BOWL. Green Agate, Chartreuse, Pearl Grey, Coral Candleholders: 11½" long. Retail Price $6.00 Pr. Bowl: 17" long. Retail Price $5.00.

R1208 BUTTERFLY CANDLEHOLDERS R1207 BUTTERFLY BOWL. Green Agate, Chartreuse, Coral Candleholders: 6½" long. Retail Price $4.00 Pr. Bowl: 14" long. Retail Price $5.00

R1220 GAZELLE BOWL. Green Agate, Chartreuse, Coral, Walnut 11" long. Retail $4.50

R1181 FLUTED CANDLEHOLDERS - R1180 RECTAN-GULAR FLUTED BOWL. Green Agate, Chartreuse, Oxblood, Mulberry Candleholders: 3½" high. Retailprice $4.00 Pr. Bowl: 11 3/4" long. Retail Price $6.00

R1234 ACANTHUS CANDLEHOLDERS - R1233 ACANTHUS BOWL. Green Agate, Chartreuse, Coral, Pearl Grey Candleholders: 7½" long. Retail $5.00 Pr. Bowl: 13½" long. Retail $4.00

Numerical Index with Price Guide

* Asterisk Indicates Picture in Photo Section
PND Indicates: Price Not Determined

R-5	Leaf Plate, Notched Top	$8.00-10.00	R-125	Flying Bird Flower Block, (Seagull-wings over head), 17½"H	$25.00-30.00
R-10	Ashtray Trio (nest 3 sizes), 8½", 6½", 4½"W	$8.00-12.00	* R-126 & 126X	Large Leaf Plate, 15"W	$6.00-8.00
F-16	Wild Goose - Wings Straight, 7"L	$6.00-8.00	R-126L	Large Leaf Plate w/divisions, 16"W	$8.00-10.00
F-17	Wild Goose - Wings up, 6½"H	$6.00-8.00	* R-126A	Leaf Plate, small, 11"W	$4.00-6.00
R-20	Cut-Out Bowl, Round, 16"W	$30.00-35.00	* R-127	Large Bowl w/Floral Cut-Outs, 13½"W	$25.00-30.00
* R-31	Peacock Vase, (Gladiola) 3 variations: Head Straight, wings down at sides and visible; Head Turned, wings down at sides and visible; and Head Straight, with NO visible side wings. (All three peacocks measure 15" high)	$40.00-45.00	R-128	Large Bowl w/Floral Cut-Outs, 14"W	$25.00-30.00
			R-129	Bowl, footed, 14"W	$10.00-12.00
			* R-130	Pheasant, long tail (also listed under Royal Haeger), 12"L	$10.00-12.00
			* R-131	Vase, Flower Basket w/Flowers, 10½"H	$18.00-20.00
* R-33	Triple Leaf Vase, 13½"H	$20.00-25.00	* R-132	Ram Book End, Head-down Curling horns, 9"H (ea)	$15.00-18.00
* R-33	Double Leaf Vase, 13½"H	$15.00-18.00	R-133	Bowl, flat, 18"W	$10.00-12.00
R-34	Fan Vase, double leaf design, 14"H	$12.00-15.00	R-133-3	Bowl, flat, w/3 Birds, 18"W	$20.00-25.00
* R-36	Swan Vase (neck-up, cut-outs around base), 16"H	$30.00-35.00	R-133-3B	Bowl, flat, w/3 Birds & Matching Bird Candleholders(R-22), 5"W	$30.00-35.00
R-36	Swan Vase (neck-down) bill on breast, solid base), 16"H	$30.00-35.00	R-134	Spiral Vase, footed, 11"H	$6.00-8.00
R-65	Oblong Bowl w/Flowers (window box), 24"L	$12.00-15.00	R-136	Bowl, oblong	$6.00-8.00
			R-137	Leaf Vase, single, 13½"H	$10.00-12.00
R-100	Vase, cylinder style, cut-out floral band around top, 14"H	$18.00-20.00	* R-138 and/or	Leaf Vase, single, 12½"H	$10.00-12.00
R-101	Rooster (head down) 12"H	$18.00-20.00	R-138	3 Leaping Fish Flower Block, 10"H	$20.00-25.00
R-102	Rooster (head up), 12"H	$18.00-20.00	R-140	Long Fluted Bowl, 18"L	$6.00-8.00
* R-103	Small Horse, (long legs), 8"H	$9.00-12.00	R-140 SB	Long Fluted Bowl w/5 sparrows on rim, 18"L	$20.00-25.00
R-104	Standing Deer Flower Block, 11½"H	$20.00-25.00	R-141	Maple Leaf Bowl, pointed edges, 14"W	$6.00-8.00
R-105	Bowl w/Flower Decoration, 12"L	$12.00-15.00	R-142	Bowl, notched edge, oblong, 16"W	$6.00-8.00
R-106	Tray, round, fluted, 16½"W	$12.00-15.00	R-143	Footed Bowl, Oblong, notched edge, 18"W	$8.00-10.00
R-107	Dragon Vase, Oblong, 12"H	$10.00-12.00	R-144	Floor Vase w/Floral Base, 20"H	PND
* R-108	Pouter Pigeon, 7½"H	$20.00-25.00	R-150	Plate, 16"W	$6.00-8.00
R-109	Plate, w/sections, 16"W	$10.00-12.00	R-152	Fluted Bowl, 12"L	$4.00-6.00
R-110	Elephant Planter, trunk out and down & circled, 11½"H	$20.00-25.00	R-153	Oriental Head, full face, 11"H	PND
R-112	Free Form Console Bowl, (matching candleholders R-185), 14"W	$10.00-12.00	R-155	Angel Fish, head-up, 5¼"H, small	$8.00-10.00
			R-156	Angel Fish, head-up, 6½"H, medium	$10.00-12.00
R-113	Vase, reticulated leaf pattern, 15"H	$18.00-20.00	R-157	Angel Fish, head-up, 7½"H, large	$12.00-15.00
R-114	Vase, open leaf, 9"H	$8.00-10.00	R-157A	3 Fish Figurines, noses down oval base, 10"H	$20.00-25.00
* R-115	Gazelle Vase, head open between ears, 13"H	$15.00-18.00	R-157B	3 Fish Flower Block (noses down), oval base, 12½"H	$25.00-28.00
R-116	Covered Duck, (2 pc. dish), 12"W	$12.00-15.00	R-158	Inebriated Duck, Fallen, 10"H	$20.00-22.00
R-117	Tropical Fish Planter, 9"H	$15.00-18.00	R-159	Inebriated Duck, Leaning, 10"H	$18.00-20.00
R-121	Footed Bowl, long, rolled top	$8.00-10.00	R-160	Inebriated Duck Upright, 10"L	$18.00-20.00
R-122	2 Handled Bowl, oblong, 20"L	$10.00-12.00	R-161	Race Horse w/jockey, 9"H	$20.00-22.00
R-124	Scalloped Bowl, 12"W	$18.00-20.00			

R-162	Double Race Horses w/jockey, 9"H	$25.00-30.00
R-164	Pheasant Hen, 6"H	$18.00-20.00
R-165	Pheasant Cock, 6"H	$18.00-20.00
R-166	Greyhound Head-down, 9"H	$20.00-25.00
R-167	Greyhound Head-up, 9"H	$20.00-25.00
R-168	Nude Torso Figurine, 14"H	$25.00-30.00
R-169	Trout (on tail), 6½"H	$8.00-10.00
R-169B	Leaping Trout Flower Block, 7"H	$10.00-15.00
R-170	Ram Head Vase, curling horns, 11"H	$20.00-25.00
R-171	Stallion, Head-up, 8"H	$15.00-18.00
R-172	Stallion, Head Straight, 8"H	$15.00-18.00
R-173	Double-branch candleholders, 9"W (ea)	$6.00-8.00
R-174	Laughing Horse Head Vase, head down, 10"H	$20.00-25.00
R-175	Oriental Head, Woman, ¾ face view, 11"H	PND
R-176	Oriental Head, man, ¾ face view, 11"H	PND
R-177	Vase, Oblong, Footed, 8½"H	$6.00-8.00
R-178	Small Horse, head-up, 4"H	$6.00-8.00
R-178D	Small Horse, Head-Down, 4"H	$6.00-8.00
R-179	Hanging Basket & Chain, Grape Motif, 9"H	$15.00-18.00
R-179	Low Oblong Bowl - Daisy Decoration	$8.00-10.00
R-180	Parrot (Macaw), 14"H	$30.00-35.00
R-181	Nude (arms & hands covering face), 14"H	PND
* R-182R	Swan Vase, right position, 8"H	$10.00-12.00
* R-182L	Swan Vase, left position, 8"H	$10.00-12.00
R-183	Candleholders, single fish, 5"H (ea)	$6.00-8.00
R-184	Boot Vase, tall, narrow, 11"H	$15.00-18.00
R-185	Leaf Candleholders, flat, 5½"W (ea)	$4.00-6.00
* R-186	Bird of Paradise Vase, large, 12¾"H	$20.00-25.00
R-187	Footed Vase, triangle shaped, squid motif, 9"H	$8.00-10.00
R-188	Cookie Jar with Lid, 10"h	$20.00-25.00
R-189	Nude Flower Block, sitting-knees up, 6"H	$18.00-20.00
R-190	Footed 4 Sided Vase, squid motif, 8"H	$8.00-10.00
R-192	Vase, Bird Perched on Vase, Wings Up, 11"H	$18.00-22.00
R-193	Vase w/rope decoration, 11"H	$8.00-10.00
R-194	Vase, circle w/point, 9"H	$6.00-8.00
R-195	Vase, side design, 9"H	$8.00-10.00
R-196	Leaf Vase, 9"H	$8.00-10.00
R-198	Bowl, round, footed, crimped top, 11½"W	$8.00-10.00
R-199	Nude, back arched on post, arms up over head, 18"H	PND
R-200	Covered Candy Box w/2 birds on lid, 5"W	$8.00-10.00
R-203	Fish Candleholder, double, 5"H (ea)	$8.00-10.00
R-205	Small Fish Planter, 6"H	$6.00-8.00
R-206	Large Fish Planter, 7"H	$8.00-10.00
R-208	Seagull Vase, (3 gulls wings up over heads), 16"H	PND
R-209	Console bowl w/2 pigeons, 19"W	$30.00-35.00
* R-210	Bowl w/2 birds, small, 7"W	$10.00-12.00
R-212	Bowl w/applied leaf, 18" W	$8.00-10.00
R-218	Two giraffe figurines, 15"H	$25.00-30.00
R-218B	Two Giraffe Flower Block, 15"H	$25.00-30.00
R-220	Candleholders/2 Birds, 5½"H (ea)	$6.00-8.00
R-221	Frog Sitting on Beehive Style Vase, 12"H	$18.00-20.00
R-222	Frog Sitting on Round Spiral Vase, 12"H	$18.00-20.00
* R-223	Lily Bowl w/3 lillies, small, 7"W	$8.00-10.00
* R-224	Daisy Bowl, 12"W	$12.00-15.00
R-225	Footed Bowl, 6"W	$6.00-8.00
R-226	Bowl, Piecrust Edge, 8"W	$6.00-8.00
R-227	Lily Bowl w/3 lilies, large, 13"W	$10.00-12.00
* R-228	Cornucopia Vase, 12"H	$15.00-18.00
R-229	2 Cockatoo Vase, Square Column, 15"H	$20.00-25.00
* R-230	Cog Wheel Ashtray, 7"W	$4.00-5.00
R-231	Floor Vase, prancing deer border in relief, 23"H	PND
R-232	Round planter, prancing deer in relief, 8"H	$8.00-10.00
R-233	Pouter Pigeon, 7"H	$18.00-20.00
R-234	Colt, long legs, figurine, 12"H	$20.00-22.00
* R-235	Colt, long legs, flower holder (head-down), 12½"H	$20.00-22.00
R-237	3 Ducks/Geese - wings down, beaks out, 11"H	$20.00-25.00
R-238	3 Fish Planter, (curved backs), 8"H	$15.00-18.00
R-241	Yacha Vase, 15"H	$18.00-20.00
R-242	Frog Sitting on Low Bowl, 13½"W	$20.00-22.00
R-243	Vase, cylinder shape w/square Pedestal, 12"	$8.00-10.00
* R-246	Double Cornucopia Vase, 16"L	$20.00-25.00
R-247	Swan Vase, beak on breast, in waves, 12½"H	$20.00-25.00
* R-248	Plume Feather Console Vase, 10"H	$12.00-15.00
R-251	Onion Jug Vase, 21"H	$15.00-18.00
R-252	Square Ashtray, 7"W	$4.00-5.00
R-255	Vase	$6.00-8.00
* R-256	Jardinier with curled edge, 12"D	PND
R-270	Tropical Fish on Waves, (Also in BOKO finish), 15"H	$35.00-40.00
* R-271	Sail Fish Vase, 9"H	$20.00-22.00
R-273	Spanish Senor Vase	$10.00-12.00
R-274	Spanish Senorita Vase	$10.00-12.00
* R-277	Small Spiral Plume Dish, 6"W	$8.00-10.00
R-278	Large Spiral Plume Dish, 9"W	$10.00-12.00
R-279	Basket Vase, 21"H	PND
* R-281	Sphere & 3 Plumes, 10½"H	$25.00-30.00
R-282	Oblong bowl, footed, 10½"L	$10.00-12.00
R-282X	Oblong Bowl (Ebony) Footed, 10½"L	$10.00-12.00
* R-284	Trout Flower Vase, 7"H	$15.00-18.00
* R-285	Swan Vase, 9"H	$10.00-12.00
* R-286	Leaf Plate, 12"L	$8.00-10.00
* R-287	Bird House w/2 birds, 9½"H	$12.00-15.00
* R-290	Cut Out "V" Bowl, 10"W	$12.00-15.00
R-291	Bowl	$6.00-8.00
* R-293	Violin Bowl, 17"L	$12.00-14.00
* R-295	Plume Candleholder, 4"H (ea)	$4.00-6.00
R-297	Oval Shell Bowl, footed, 7½"L	$6.00-8.00
* R-298	Cornucopia Shell Vase, 11"L	$15.00-18.00
* R-299	Snail Shell Vase, 11"L	$10.00-12.00
* R-301	Double Leaf Fan Vase, 9½"H	$8.00-10.00
* R-303	Laurel Wreath Bow Vase, 12"H	$15.00-18.00
R-304	Fish Candleholder, 4¼"H (ea)	$6.00-8.00
R-305	Giraffe (or Gazelle) Head on Oblong Stand, 19"H	PND
R-306	Plume Shell Bowl, 15"L	$15.00-18.00
R-307	Round Bowl, 11"L	$6.00-8.00

R-308	4-Footed Bowl, 12″W	$6.00-8.00	* R-370	Dutch Cup Bowl, 19″L	$8.00-10.00
* R-309	Ruching Bowl, 14½″L	$8.00-10.00	R-371	Low Wave Bowl, (Whirling Bowl), 13″L	$8.00-10.00
* R-310	Large Swan Bowl, 13″L	$15.00-18.00	* R-372	Round Fluted Bowl, 13½″W	$8.00-10.00
* R-312	Cornucopia Candleholder, 5½″H (ea)	$4.00-6.00	* R-373	Console Bowl, long, curved with applied fruit on sides, 20″L	$25.00-30.00
R-313	Tigress Figurine, 8″H	$30.00-35.00	* R-375A	Polar Bear Cub sitting, 3″H	$6.00-8.00
R-313X	Tigress Figurine (Ebony), 8″H	$30.00-35.00	R-375B	Polar Bear "sitting", 7″L	$10.00-15.00
R-314	Tiger Figurine, 11″H	$30.00-35.00	R-376A	Polar Bear Cub, standing, 2½″H	$6.00-8.00
* R-314X	Tiger Figurine (Ebony), 11″H	$30.00-35.00	* R-376B	Polar Bear, standing, 5½″L	$10.00-15.00
R-315	Girl Figurine, Kneeling, 12″L	$15.00-20.00	R-377	Cabbage Rose Vase, 16″H	$20.00-25.00
R-316	3 Bird Flower Holder, 8″L	$10.00-12.00	R-379	Bull on Square Base, 7½″H	$25.00-30.00
R-317	Anchor Vase, 10″H	$8.00-10.00	R-382	Peasant Figurine, female, 17″H	$30.00-35.00
R-318	Russian Wolfhound head-down, 7″L	$22.00-25.00	R-382	Peasant Figurine, male, 17″H	$30.00-35.00
* R-319	Russian Wolfhound head-up, 7″L	$22.00-25.00	* R-386	Basket vase with floral border (triangular shape), 12″L	$15.00-18.00
R-320	Elm Leaf Vase, 12″H	$8.00-10.00	R-387	Tall Modern Vase, footed, 16″H	$12.00-15.00
* R-321	Conch Shell Vase, 8″H	$8.00-10.00	R-390	South American Girl, (from neck up), 11″H	$30.00-35.00
* R-322	Double Shell Cornucopia Vase, 7½″H	$15.00-18.00	R-391	African Man w/bananas, (from arms up) 12″H	$30.00-35.00
R-322B	Cornucopia, straight, vase, 11″H	$15.00-18.00	* R-393	Bust of Pegasus Vase, 11¼″H	$20.00-25.00
R-322C	Cornucopia, straight, vase (fluted), 16″H	$20.00-22.00	R-397	3 Block Candleholder, 8″L (ea)	$7.00-8.00
R-323	Corrugated Vase, 9″H	$6.00-8.00	R-400	Rooster, 5″H	$6.00-8.00
R-324	Ribbed Concave Vase, 10″H	$6.00-8.00	R-401	Hen, 4″H	$6.00-8.00
R-326	Round Fluted Bowl on Base, 11″W	$6.00-8.00	* R-402	Dappled Horse, 6″H	$8.00-10.00
R-328	Bowl oval, plume feet, 6″H	$12.00-15.00	R-403	Man w/bananas on head, 13½″H	$30.00-35.00
R-329	Conch Shell Bowl, 7″L	$8.00-10.00	R-404	Woman w/fruit basket on head, 12½″H	$30.00-35.00
* R-332A	Ornate Cornucopia Vase, 8″H	$10.00-12.00	R-406	Calla Lily Vase w/appld dec., 13″H	$18.00-20.00
R-332B	Ornate Cornucopia Vase, large, 11″H	$15.00-18.00	* R-407	Wren House w/1 bird, 6½″H	$6.00-8.00
R-333B	Lady Flower Block, 15¼″H	30.00-35.00	R-408	Double Racing Horses, 10″H	$20.00-25.00
R-334	Fan Tail Pigeon Vase, 9″H	$25.00-30.00	R-409	Pillow Vase w/flowers, 11½″H	$8.00-10.00
R-335	Shell Bowl, 14″W	$15.00-20.00	R-410	Wheat Sheaf Vase, 12″H	$15.00-18.00
R-337	Urn w/Beaded Base, 11″H	$6.00-8.00	R-411	Girl w/doe, 10½″H	$30.00-35.00
R-340	Pedestal Bowl, footed	$6.00-8.00	* R-412	Standing Fawn, 11½″H	$8.00-10.00
R-341	Bowl, round, footed, on Base, 14″W	$6.00-8.00	* R-413	Kneeling Fawn, 7½″H	$6.00-8.00
R-342	Handled Vase, 12½″H	$8.00-10.00	* R-414	Swan, head-down, 12″W	$22.00-25.00
R-343	Petal Bowl, 8″H	$4.00-5.00	R-415	Big Horse, 13″L	$30.00-35.00
R-345	Pedestal Vase w/running deer, 9″H	$12.00-15.00	R-416	Plain Urn w/bird cover, 13½″H	$18.00-20.00
R-346	Sectional Tray, 6 sections and center, 17″W	$15.00-18.00	R-418	Dbl. Candleholder, 9″L	$7.00-9.00
R-347	Angelfish planter w/mermaid on back, 13″H	$20.00-25.00	R-420	Footed Console Bowl w/candlesticks, 11″H	$20.00-22.00
R-349	Vase, 9″H	$6.00-8.00	* R-421	Pedestal Bowl w/grape clusters, 14″W	$20.00-25.00
R-350	Pheasants on Pedestal, 14″L	$18.00-20.00	* R-422	Cornucopia Vase, 6″H	$7.00-9.00
* R-351	Squat Urn, (Shorter Modern Vase), 10¼″H	$10.00-12.00	* R-424	Bucking Horse & Cowboy, 13″H	$25.00-30.00
R-353	Tall Compote w/wreath on top, 10″H	$8.00-10.00	R-425	Parrot on Vase (Macaw)	$35.00-40.00
R-355	2 Leaf Vase, 10¼″H	$8.00-10.00	* R-426	Cornucopia w/nude kneeling, 8″H	$15.00-18.00
R-356	Chalice Vase, 12″H	$10.00-12.00	R-427	Sitting Horse Vase, 11″H	$15.00-18.00
R-357	Low Fluted Bowl, 16″L	$6.00-8.00	R-428	Onion Jug w/petal opening, 17″H	$10.00-12.00
* R-358	Footed Bowl, 18″L	$10.00-12.00	* R-430	Swan Vase, 8″H	$8.00-10.00
* R-359	2 Bird Flower Block, 11″W	$18.00-20.00	* R-431	Calla Lily Candy Box, 7½″W	$8.00-10.00
* R-360	2 Tropical Fish Flower Block, 11″H	$18.00-20.00	R-432	Shell Bowl, 9″H	$8.00-10.00
* R-361	3 Birds on Branch Block, 7″L	$10.00-15.00	R-433	Triple Candleholders, wave-style, 11½″L (ea)	$10.00-12.00
R-362	Lady Standing Flower Block, 12″H	$20.00-25.00	R-434	Hen Pheasant, 12″L	$18.00-22.00
* R-363	Nude Astride Fish Flower Block, 10″H	$18.00-20.00	R-435	Rooster Pheasant, 12″H	$18.00-22.00
* R-364	Nude with Seal, Flower Block, 13″H	$25.00-30.00	R-436	Flower Pot, oblong, w/flowers, 7½″L	$4.00-5.00
R-366	Bowl on Base, 6″H	$6.00-8.00	R-437	Leaf Candleholder, 5″L (ea)	$4.00-6.00
R-367	Spiral Vase, 12″H	$6.00-8.00	R-438	Rose Bud Candleholder, 3½″W	$4.00-6.00 ea.
R-368	Candle Stick, 16″H	$15.00-18.00 ea.	R-439	Bow Console Bowl, 12½″L	$8.00-10.00
R-369	Standing Shell Bowl, 14″H	$12.00-15.00	R-440	Bow Candleholders, 5″L	$4.00-6.00 ea.
			R-441	Circular, Art Deco Vase, 11½″H	$15.00-18.00
			R-442	Bowl w/floral pattern, 18″L	$8.00-10.00
			R-443	Coolie Hat Bowl, 16½″W	$8.00-10.00
			R-444	Upright Leaf Vase, 6½″H	$4.00-6.00
			R-445	Flower Pot, 4½″H	$4.00-6.00

* R-446	Lily Vase, 14"H	$20.00-22.00
R-447	Shell Ashtray, 4½"W	$2.00-3.00
R-448	Small Shell Dish, 3½"W	$3.00-4.00
R-449	Leaf Ashtray, 5"L	$3.00-4.00
R-450	Long Narrow Bowl w/floral design, 23"L	$8.00-10.00
R-451	Mare & Foal, standing, 13½"L	$25.00-30.00
* R-452	Morning Glory Vase w/3 flower openings, 16"H	$20.00-22.00
* R-453	Small Peacock Vase, 10"H	$12.00-15.00
R-454	Chinese Vase, 15"H	$12.00-14.00
* R-455	Tall Bow Vase, 15"H	$15.00-20.00
* R-456	Wrap Around Spiral Vase, 13"H	$15.00-20.00
R-457	3 Leaf Dish w/bird in center, 9"L	$10.00-12.00
R-458	3 Shell Candy Dish w/bird, small, 6½"L	$8.00-10.00
R-459	3 Shell Candy Dish w/bird, large, 9"L	$10.00-12.00
R-460	Console Leaf Bowl w/floral base, 12"L	$12.00-15.00
* R-466	Long Curving Bowl, 15"L	$6.00-8.00
R-467	Flying Goose Vase, 16¼"L	$25.00-30.00
R-468	Candlestick, 16½"H (ea)	$15.00-18.00
R-469	Bowl, 12"L	$8.00-10.00
R-470	Fluted Bowl, 12"W	$6.00-8.00
* R-472	Russian Lady's Head, 12"H	$30.00-35.00
* R-473	Twin Stalk Candleholder, 10"H (ea)	$12.00-15.00
R-474	Vase w/applied flowers, 9"H	$10.00-12.00
* R-475	Calla Lily Bookends, 6"H (pr)	$15.00-20.00
* R-476	Beaded Bowl, 15"L	$6.00-8.00
R-477	Modernistic Lady's Head, 13½"H	$30.00-35.00
* R-479	Prospector w/burros, 11½"L	$18.00-20.00
R-480	Pegasus Vase, 10½"H	$20.00-25.00
* R-481	Sea Shell on Base, 11¼"H	$18.00-20.00
* R-482	Plume Vase, large 14"H	$20.00-22.00
* R-483	Upright Shell, 11"H	$15.00-18.00
R-484	Miniature Garden Bowl, 13"L	$8.00-10.00
* R-485	Upright Candleholders, 7½"L (ea)	$4.00-5.00
R-486	Square Bowl, 9½"W	$6.00-8.00
R-487	Triangular Bowl, 8¼"H	$6.00-8.00
R-488	Pillow Vase, 7½"H	$6.00-8.00
R-489	Tropical Leaf Vase, 13"H	$8.00-10.00
R-490	Triangular Vase, 15"H	$10.00-12.00
R-491	Ram's Head on black square base, 12"H	$20.00-25.00
R-492	Modernistic Horsehead Vase, 15½"H	$25.00-30.00
* R-493	Egyptian Cat head down, 6½"H	$10.00-12.00
R-494	Egyptian Cat, head up, 7½"H	$10.00-12.00
R-495	Black Panther, Tail Out & Down, 26"L	PND
R-495	Black Panther Tail Curled, 24"L	$25.00-30.00
* R-496	Bud Vase, 8"H	$5.00-8.00
R-497	Roman Vase, 9½"H	$6.00-8.00
R-498	Roman Vase, Bas-Relief Flowers, 9¼"H	$8.00-10.00
R-499	Decorated Bowl, 8"W	$8.00-10.00
R-500	Bee Hive Vase, Grapes & Leaves, 7½"H	$8.00-10.00
R-501	Bee Hive Vase w/flowers, 7"H	$6.00-8.00
R-502	Roman Vase, 7½"H	$6.00-8.00
R-503	Plain Oval Vase, 7¼"H	$6.00-8.00
R-504	Bee Hive Vase, 6"H	$6.00-8.00
R-505	Tulip Vase, 5"H	$6.00-8.00
R-506	Tulip Vase, 7½"H	$8.00-10.00
R-507	Tulip Vase, 10"H	$10.00-12.00
R-508	Dolphin Vase, 18"H	$20.00-25.00
R-509	Large Dolphin Bowl, 20"W	$15.00-20.00
R-510	Small Dolphin Bowl, 15"W	$10.00-12.00
R-511	Dolphin Candleholder, 10¾"H	$10.00-12.00
R-512	Dolphin Candy Dish, 7½"W	$12.00-15.00
R-513	Dolphin Ashtray, 6"L	$6.00-8.00
R-514	Dolphin Flower Block, 9¾"H	$15.00-20.00
R-515	Swan Bowl, 17½"W	$18.00-20.00
* R-516	Swan Candleholders, 8"H	$10.00-12.00
R-517	Swan Wall Pocket, 9"H	$8.00-10.00
R-518	Swan Ashtray, 7¾"W	$6.00-8.00
R-519	Swan Vase, 11½"	$15.00-18.00
R-520	Bamboo Ashtray, Triangle style, 8½"W	$4.00-6.00
R-521	Bamboo Vase, raised design, 15"H	$8.00-10.00
R-522	Bamboo Bowl, low, oblong, 16½"W	$8.00-10.00
* R-523	Fan Vase, 16½"W	$15.00-18.00
R-525	Double Tulip Flower Pot, 10"W	$6.00-8.00
R-526	Pillow Vase, 6"H	$5.00-7.00
R-527	Pillow Vase, 7"H	$6.00-8.00
R-528	Laurel Pillow Vase, 8"H	$8.00-9.00
R-529	Laurel Pillow Vase, 10"H	$8.00-9.00
R-530	Laurel Pillow Vase, 12"H	$9.00-10.00
R-534	Horn of Plenty, 18"L	$10.00-12.00
R-539	Elephant, 9"H	$18.00-20.00
R-540	Turtle Planter, 13½"L	$15.00-18.00
R-541	Turtle Planter, 7½"W	$8.00-10.00
* R-546	Flower Candleholders (round & flat) (ea)	$4.00-5.00
R-555	Pei Tung Vase, 13½"H	$8.00-10.00
R-556	Laurel Bowl Console "Footed", 11"H	$10.00-12.00
R-558	Laurel Candleholders, 5"H (ea)	$3.00-4.00
R-559	Laurel Ashtray, 6½"W	$2.00-3.00
* R-560	Laurel Cig. Box, 7"L, w/lid	$6.00-9.00
R-561	Dragon Bowl, 10"L	$10.00-12.00
R-562	Pei Tung Bowl, 9½"W	$8.00-10.00
R-563	Elephant Planter, 10½"H	$20.00-25.00
R-567	Leaf Ashtray, 8"W	$5.00-7.00
R-568	Octopus Bowl, shallow, 16"W	$10.00-12.00
R-570	Pei Tung Dragon, 15¼"H	$25.00-30.00
R-571	Jeweled Lady, flower block, 15½"H	$20.00-22.00
R-573	Low Bowl, 12½"W	$6.00-8.00
R-575	Rose of Sharon Basket, 7"H	$15.00-18.00
R-577	Rose of Sharon Cig. Box, 8"L	$10.00-12.00
* R-579	2 Block Candleholder, 5"L (ea)	$4.00-6.00
* R-580	Rose of Sharon Vase, 9¼"H	$12.00-15.00
R-583	Pitcher, 8"H	$8.00-10.00
R-584	Creamer, 5"H	$4.00-6.00
R-585	Sugar, 5¼"H	$4.00-6.00
R-586	Mug, 4½"H	$4.00-6.00
* R-590	Hawaiian Candy Box, 2 pc. (round), 8"W	$18.00-20.00
R-594	Rose of Sharon Ashtray, 6"W	$6.00-8.00
* R-595	Fish Pitcher, 9"H	$15.00-18.00
* R-596	Barn Yard Riders, (Horse w/3 riders), 14"L	$75.00-85.00
R 597	Leaf Ashtray, 6"W	$2.00-3.00
R-598	Leaf Candleholder, 6"L (ea)	$4.00-5.00
R-599	Console Bowl, 19"L	$8.00-10.00
R-600	Woodsman w/axe bud vase, 9"H	$10.00-12.00
R-601	Woodsman Wife Bud Vase, 7"H	$8.00-10.00
R-602	Woodsman Boy Bud Vase, 5½"H	$6.00-8.00
R-603	Goldi Locks Bud Vase, 5½"H	$6.00-8.00
R-604	Bear w/tree trunk, 5½"H	$6.00-8.00
R-605	Shell Abstract Vase	$6.00-8.00
R-611	Fish Console Dish, 12"L	$8.00-10.00
R-612	Fish Abstract Tray w/tail, 8½"L	$6.00-8.00
R-613	Fish Abstract w/out tail, 5½"L	$4.00-6.00
R-614	Scroll Bowl, 14½"L	$10.00-12.00
R-616	Tulip Vase, 8"H	$8.00-10.00

R-618	Thought Figurine	PND
R-621	Chinese Planter, 8"L	$6.00-8.00
R-622	Chinese Candleholder (figures), 5"H (ea)	$8.00-10.00
R-624	2 Does, Heads & Necks, Large & Small, 14½"H	$20.00-25.00
R-625	Elephant Cig. Box, 3 elephant lid, 8¼"L	$15.00-18.00
R-627	Chinese Bowl, 10½"L	$6.00-8.00
* R-628	Chinese Lady (Also #1015), 6"H	$6.00-8.00
* R-629	Chinese Man (Also #1015), 5½"H	$6.00-8.00
R-631	Small Leopard Cig. Box, 7"L	$18.00-20.00
R-632	Small Leopard Ashtray, 8½"W	$18.00-20.00
R-633	Imperial Mongolian Man, 23"H	PND
R-634	Imperial Mongolian Woman, 23½"H	PND
R-635	Pei Tung Planter, 15"L	$8.00-10.00
R-638	Leopard Bookend Planter, 15"L (ea)	$20.00-25.00
R-639	Leopard Circus Planter, 12½"L	$40.00-45.00
* R-641	Stallion Bookend Planter, 8½"H	$10.00-12.00
* R-646	Tulip Vase, 8"H	$8.00-10.00
* R-647	Sun Flower Vase, 8"H	$8.00-10.00
R-648	Sitting Leopard, 6"H	$8.00-10.00
* R-649	Lying Leopard, 7"L	$8.00-10.00
R-650	Oblong Bowl, 9½"L	$6.00-8.00
* R-651	Pillow Vase, 8"H	$6.00-8.00
R-652	Floral Vase, 7½"H	$8.00-10.00
R-653	Zephyr Vase, 8"H	$8.00-10.00
R-654	Oval Rose Bowl, 17"L	$8.00-10.00
R-655	Fish Globe Stand - Frog Fishing, 12½"L	$30.00-35.00
R-656	Fish Globe Stand - Mermaid, 11½"H	$30.00-35.00
* R-657	Gondolier Planter, with inserts, 19½"L	$18.00-20.00
R-658	Fish & Waves Vase, 14"H	$10.00-12.00
R-659	Alligator Vase, 14½"H	$10.00-12.00
R-660	Birds & Sprigs Vase, 14"H	$10.00-12.00
R-663	Sq. Cube Planter Pot, 7"H	$5.00-7.00
* R-664	Polar Bear Candy Box, 7½"W	$18.00-20.00
R-665	Plain Vase, tall w base, 10"H	$6.00-8.00
R-666	Plain Bowl, round, low, w/base, 9"W	$4.00-6.00
R-667	Plain Vase, round w/collar, 8½"H	$6.00-8.00
R-668	Small Elephant Ashtray—1 elephant, 4"W	$6.00-8.00
R-669	Cube Checked Cig. Box, sea urchin finial, 7"L	$10.00-12.00
R-670	Cube Checked Ashtray, 5¼"W	$4.00-6.00
R-671	Candleholder, 6"W (ea)	$4.00-6.00
R-672	Mongolian Man Flower Block, 12½"H	$15.00-20.00
R-673	Mongolian Woman Flower Block, 13"H	$15.00-20.00
R-679	Round Bowl Console, 12"W	$6.00-8.00
R-680	Round Candleholders, 5"H (ea)	$4.00-6.00
R-681	Rectangular Bowl, 14½"L	$7.00-9.00
R-682	Candleholders (double socket), 7"L (ea)	$6.00-8.00
* R-683	Panther, 18"L	$15.00-20.00
* R-684	Turtle Cig. Box, 9¼"L w/lid	$12.00-15.00
R-685	Horse Head Cig. Box, 7"L	$12.00-18.00
R-686	Horse Head Ashtray, 8"W	$6.00-8.00
R-687	Fish Cig. Box, 4½"L	$8.00-10.00
R-688	Fish Ashtray, 4"W	$4.00-5.00
R-688X	Fish Cig. Box w/2 ashtrays (complete)	$15.00-18.00
R-689	Sq. Shallow Box, 10½"W	$5.00-8.00
* R-690	Sq. Chinese Candleholder, 5"W (ea)	$5.00-6.00
R-691	Sq. Vase w/side trim, 15"H	$8.00-10.00
R-692	Round Bowl, 12½"W	$6.00-8.00
R-692A	Stand for R-692	$6.00-8.00
R-692B	Round Bowl & Stand, 12½"W	$12.00-15.00
R-693	Wrap Around Vase, 18"H	$20.00-25.00
R-694	Buddha, 10½"H	$20.00-25.00
R-695	Lion Figurine	$30.00-35.00
R-697	Swirl Vase	$6.00-8.00
R-698	Mexican Head Pitcher, 7"H	$15.00-18.00
R-699	Mexican Mug, 4"H	$4.00-6.00
R-700	Lion Head Bookends, 7½"H (pr)	$20.00-25.00
* R-701	Sea Shell Vase, 11"H	$12.00-14.00
R-702	Polar Bear, 16"L	$25.00-30.00
R-705	Fish Vase	$8.00-10.00
* R-706	Running Deer Vase, 15"H	$18.00-22.00
* R-707	Standing Deer Vase, 15"H	$18.00-22.00
R-708	Pigeon Vase	$8.00-10.00
R-709	Sm. Horn of Plenty, 12½"L	$8.00-10.00
R-710	Sq. Flower Block	$6.00-8.00
R-711	Chinese Musician, 11"H	$18.00-20.00
* R-712	Bird of Paradise, 9"H	$15.00-18.00 ea.
* R-713	Swan Vase, 8"H	$10.00-12.00
* R-714	Fan Vase, 9½"L	$6.00-8.00
R-715	Fruit Flower Basket (compote style)	$18.00-22.00
* R-716	Bud Vase, 9"H	$5.00-8.00
* R-718	Ram Head Bookends, 5½"H	$18.00-22.00 pr
R-719	Lg. Fish Planter	$25.00-30.00
R-720	Ming Horse	$18.00-22.00
R-721	Indian on Horse	$25.00-30.00
R-722	Lg. Prospector	$20.00-25.00
R-723	Feather Vase, 8½"H	$15.00-18.00
R-724	Rocking Horse Wall Pocket	$8.00-10.00
R-725	Rect. Wall Pocket, 5"H	$6.00-8.00
* R-727	Hex. Low Bowl, 12"W	$6.00-8.00
R-727S	Bowl, Candle, Holders & Flower Block	$25.00-28.00
R-728	Oval Bowl, long, w/raised flowers	$15.00-18.00
R-728S	Bowl, Candle Holders & Flower Block	$25.00-28.00
R-729	Candle Holder (ea)	$4.00-6.00
R-730	Flower Block	$6.00-8.00
R-731	4-Sectional Tray	$12.00-15.00
R-732	Leaf Vase with twisted rope-like branch	$10.00-12.00
* R-733	Panther, 13"L	$12.00-15.00
R-734	Collie Figurine	$20.00-25.00
R-735	Cocker Spaniel Figurine, 9"h	$20.00-25.00
R-735S	Cocker w/4 pups	$50.00-55.00
* R-736	Dachshund Figurine, 14½"L	$18.00-22.00
R-737	Petunia Bowl	$8.00-10.00
R-737S	Bowl & Candle holders	$20.00-25.00
R-738	Candle holder (ea)	$6.00-8.00
R-739	Horse & Colt (head & neck)	$20.00-25.00
R-740	Giraffe & Young, (head & neck)	$20.00-25.00
R-741	Indian Bookend Planter (pr)	$20.00-25.00
R-742	Fish & Waves Vase	$12.00-15.00
R-743	Conch Shell Vase	$8.00-10.00
R-744	Horse Head Vase	$18.00-20.00
R-745	Grape Vine Wall Pocket	$7.00-9.00
R-746	Rd. Leaf Bowl	$6.00-8.00
R-746S	Bowl & Candle Holders	$18.00-20.00
R-747	Leaf Candle Holders (ea)	$4.00-6.00
R-748	Small Bowl	$4.00-6.00
R-749	3 Compartment Clover Dish	$4.00-6.00
R-750	Fish Planter, 5½"H	$6.00-8.00
R-751	Fish Planter, 6½"H	$8.00-10.00
* R-752	Fish Planter, 8½"H	$10.00-12.00
R-753	Grape Vine Basket, hanging with chain	$15.00-18.00

* R-754	Donkey Cart Planter, 11¼"L	$10.00-12.00	
R-755	Modern Form Bowl, 14"W	$8.00-10.00	
R-755S	Bowl & Candle Holders	$15.00-20.00	
R-756	Modern Candle Holders, 5½"H (ea)	$4.00-5.00	
* R-757	Hex. Candle Holders, 5"W (ea)	$4.00-6.00	
R-758	Egyptian Cat	$20.00-25.00	
R-759	Temple Goddess	$18.00-22.00	
R-760	Leopard Planter	$25.00-30.00	
R-761	Hex. Flower Block	$4.00-6.00	
R-762	Daisy Pot	$4.00-6.00	
R-763	Lilac Pot	$4.00-6.00	
R-764	Tulip Pot	$4.00-6.00	
R-765	Saucer & Pot	$4.00-6.00	
* R-766	Rudolph The Red Nosed Reindeer (Planter and/or Lamp), 9½"h	PND	
R-767	Madonna	$8.00-10.00	
R-768	Holy Water Fount	PND	
R-769	Leaf Vase (very fancy)	$8.00-10.00	
R-770	Flared Bowl (vase), 13"W	$10.00-12.00	
* R-771	Leaf Bowl, 15"L	$6.00-8.00	
R-771S	Leaf Bowl & Stag Figurines, 15"L	$20.00-25.00	
R-772	Stag Flower Block	$15.00-18.00	
R-773	Scroll Vase, 10"H	$7.00-9.00	
R-774	Triple Rustic Candle Holder (ea)	$9.00-12.00	
R-775	Sail Ship	PND	
* R-776	Sleeping Cocker Pup, 6"L	$6.00-8.00	
R-777	Standing Cocker Pup, 4¾"H	$6.00-8.00	
R-778	Rolling Cocker Pup, 6"L	$6.00-8.00	
R-779	Begging Cocker Pup, 4"H	$6.00-8.00	
R-780	Mister Scot	$18.00-22.00	
R-781	Miss Peke	$12.00-15.00	
R-782	Shetland Puppies (3 in group)	$12.00-15.00	
R-783	Elephant figurine, 7"H	$12.00-15.00	
R-784	Elephant, 6"H	$8.00-10.00	
* R-785	Elephant figurine, 5"H	$6.00-8.00	
R-786	Modern Vase	$6.00-8.00	
R-787	Race Track Oval Bowl, 14"L	$8.00-10.00	
R-787S	Oval Bowl & Jockey Flower Block, 14"L	$20.00-25.00	
R-788	Jockey Flower Block	$18.00-20.00	
R-789	Triangle Fish Vase with seaweed, 14½"H	$12.00-15.00	
* R-790	Fighting Cock, left, 11½"H	$20.00-22.00	
* R-791	Fighting Cock, right, 11½"H	$20.00-22.00	
R-792	Open Bowl w/flower block, 17"W	$12.00-15.00	
R-792S	Open Bowl, Flower Blk., Candle Holders, 17"W	$20.00-25.00	
* R-793	Candle Holder for Open Bowl, 7"H (ea)	$4.00-6.00	
R-794	Rustic Bookends (pr)	$15.00-18.00	
R-795	Scroll Bookends (pr)	$15.00-18.00	
R-796	Fae Huttenlocher Bowl	$6.00-8.00	
R-796A	Stand for R-796	$6.00-8.00	
R-796B	Bowl & Stand 14"W x 3½"H	$10.00-12.00	
R-797	Fae Huttenlocher Rect. Rustic Bowl	$5.00-6.00	
R-798	Lg. Rect. Bowl	$5.00-6.00	
R-799	Bamboo Bowl	$5.00-6.00	
R-801	Claycraft Bowl, 12"L	$6.00-8.00	
R-804	Claycraft Tray, 5½"W	$4.00-6.00	
R-805	Claycraft Candy Dish, 8½"W	$5.00-7.00	
R-807	Rustic Bowl (Fae Huttenlocher)	$5.00-6.00	
R-808	Mountain Lion	$30.00-35.00	
* R-809	Gazelle Planter, 14"H	$25.00-30.00	
R-810	Lazy Susan	$8.00-10.00	
R-811	Palette Ashtray, 9½"L	$6.00-8.00	
* R-812	Gondola (no inserts), 15½"L	$8.00-10.00	
R-813	Flower Block for R-792	$6.00-8.00	
* R-816	Petal Bowl w/ebony base, 10"L	$8.00-10.00	
* R-819	Acanthus Leaf Bowl, 14"L	$8.00-10.00	
R-820	Bird Block for bowl, 7"	$10.00-15.00	
* R-821	Lg. Oval Leaf Bowl w/appld. fruit, 19"L	$22.00-25.00	
R-822	Fish Abstract Box	$6.00-8.00	
R-823	Abstract Ashtray	$4.00-6.00	
R-824	Oblong Cig. Box	$6.00-8.00	
R-826	Modern Vase, 9"H	$6.00-8.00	
R-827	Modern Vase (wraparound), 10"H	$8.00-10.00	
R-830	Scroll Vase, 20"H	PND	
R-831	Resting Stag Planter, 15"L	$12.00-15.00	
* R-832	Flat Sided Vase, 9"H	$10.00-12.00	
R-833	Flat Sided Vase, 12"H	$8.00-10.00	
* R-834	Turtle Planter, 11"L	$15.00-18.00	
R-835	Sm. Turtle Candleholders (ea)	$8.00-10.00	
R-836	Sitting Frog Flower Block	$10.00-12.00	
R-837	Lying Frog Flower Block	$10.00-12.00	
* R-838	Turning Frog Flower Block, 4½"L	$10.00-12.00	
R-839	Lg. Setting Duck Vase, 12"H	$20.00-25.00	
* R-840	Lg. Flying Duck Vase, 12"H	$20.00-25.00	
R-841	Tall Flamingo Vase	PND	
R-842	Pipe Ash tray	$6.00-8.00	
R-843	Oval Console Bowl, 17"L	$12.00-15.00	
R-844	Bird Wings Down	$6.00-8.00	
R-845	Bird Wings Up	$6.00-8.00	
R-846	Rooster	$15.00-18.00	
R-847	Hen, Pheasant (also R-164), 6"	$15.00-18.00	
R-848	Swirl Abstract	$6.00-8.00	
R-849	Swirl Cig. Box	$6.00-8.00	
R-851	Oblong Window Box, 10"L	$7.00-9.00	
R-852	Triple Ball Planter, 11"L	$12.00-15.00	
R-853	Vertical Lined Vase, 10"H	$6.00-8.00	
R-854	Cut Glass Vase "Crescent", 7½"L	$8.00-10.00	
R-855	Leaf Vase, 4"H	$6.00-8.00	
* R-856	Tall Swan Vase, 13"H	$15.00-20.00	
* R-857	Gazelle Head, 12"H	$15.00-18.00	
R-858	Snail Bowl	$6.00-8.00	
R-859	Cornucopia	$8.00-10.00	
R-860	Trio Ashtray, 7½"L	$5.00-6.00	
R-862	Triangle Ashtray, 7"L	$5.00-6.00	
R-863	Open Cig. Bowl (set/w R-864), 3½"L	$8.00-10.00	
R-864	Ashtray (set/w R-863), 7"W	$3.00-4.00	
R-865	Low Bowl	$5.00-6.00	
R-866	Lily Bowl	$6.00-8.00	
R-867	Pheasant, 11"L	$10.00-12.00	
R-868	Candleholders (ea)	$4.00-6.00	
* R-869	Gazelle Planter, 14"H	$25.00-30.00	
R-870	Open Bowl w/out insert	$6.00-8.00	
R-873	Free Form Ash Bowl, 8½"L	$5.00-6.00	
R-874	Sm. Colt Planter	$8.00-10.00	
R-875	Colt Planter, 14"L	$30.00-35.00	
R-876	Free Form Figure Eight Bowl, 14"L	$10.00-12.00	
R-877	Open Leaf Bowl, 14"L	$8.00-10.00	
R-878	Oyster Shell Vase, 9"H	$8.00-10.00	
R-879	Flat Sided Acanthus Leaf Vase, 7"H	$10.00-12.00	
R-880	Resting Stag Figurine, 14½"L	$15.00-18.00	
R-881	Resting Stag Planter, 18½"L	$18.00-22.00	
R-882	Double Racing Horse Figurine, 11"L	$25.00-30.00	
* R-883	Dbl. Racing Horse Planter, 18"L	$25.00-30.00	
R-884	Free Form Vase, 18"H	$10.00-12.00	
R-885	Free Form Vase, 12"H	$8.00-10.00	
* R-886	Flat Sided Free Form Vase, 10"H	$8.00-10.00	
R-887	Shell Vase, 13"H	$8.00-10.00	
R-888	Goose Quills Vase, 17½"H	$15.00-18.00	
R-891	Conventional Bud Vase, 12"H	$8.00-10.00	
R-892	Modern Bud Vase, 12"H	$8.00-10.00	
R-893	Tulip Modern Vase, 12"H	$10.00-12.00	

R-894	Low Flatsided Bowl, 18″L	$10.00-12.00
R-895	Modern Vase, 11″H	$10.00-12.00
R-896	Sleeping Cat, 7″L	$15.00-18.00
R-897	Standing Cat, 7″H	$15.00-18.00
R-898	Sitting Cat, 6″H	$15.00-18.00
R-899	Palette Vase, 12½″H	$10.00-12.00
* R-900	Modern Scroll Vase, 6″H	$6.00-8.00
* R-901	Sword Fish Vase, 6″H	$8.00-10.00
R-902	Feather Fan Vase, 6″H	$8.00-10.00
R-903	Flying Duck Vase, 9″H	$15.00-18.00
* R-904	Setting Duck Vase, 9″H	$15.00-18.00
R-905	Renaissance Vase, 16″H	$10.00-12.00
* R-907	Lily Leaf Bowl, 8″W	$6.00-8.00
* R-908	Large Lily Leaf, 11″L	$8.00-10.00
R-909	Banana Leaf, 13″L	$8.00-10.00
R-910	Large Banana Leaf, 18″L	$10.00-12.00
R-911	Wine Leaf, 10″L	$6.00-8.00
R-912	Large Wine Leaf, 15″L	$7.00-9.00
R-913	Large Tropical Leaf, 14″L	$8.00-10.00
R-914	Small Tropical Leaf, 10″L	$6.00-8.00
R-915	Large Elephant Ear Leaf, 13″L	$10.00-12.00
R-916	Small Elephant Ear Leaf, 11″L	$7.00-9.00
R-917	Peter Pan Vase, 10″H	$18.00-20.00
R-944	Duck Planter, 7″W, low	$10.00-12.00
R-945	Duck Planter, 8½″H	$12.00-15.00
R-946	Upright Duckling Candleholder, 3½″H	$6.00-8.00
R-947	Duckling Candleholder, 5″L	$6.00-8.00
R-948	Flared Bowl, 15″L	$8.00-10.00
R-949	Flared Candleholders, 3½″H (ea)	$4.00-6.00
R-950	Small Draped Bowl, 7″H	$6.00-8.00
R-951	Draped Bowl, 11″H	$8.00-10.00
R-953	Low Draped Bowl, 17″L	$10.00-12.00
R-954	Draped Candleholder, 3½″H (ea)	$4.00-6.00
* R-955	Large Swan Bowl, 11″L	$18.00-20.00
R-956	Swan Bowl, small, 8″L	$10.00-12.00
R-957	Swan Soap Dish, 6″W	$8.00-10.00
R-958	Oblong Executive Ashtray, 13½″L	$7.00-9.00
* R-959	Swan Candleholder, 5¼″H (ea)	$8.00-10.00
R-960	Banana Leaf Vase, small, 10″L	$6.00-8.00
R-961	Banana Leaf Vase, medium, 14″L	$8.00-10.00
* R-962	Banana Leaf Vase, large, 18″H	$12.00-15.00
R-963	Tobacco Leaf Ashtray, 10″	$6.00-8.00
R-964	Pipe Ashtray, 10″L	$6.00-8.00
R-965	Fish Ashtray, 9½″L	$8.00-10.00
R-967	Star Fish Bowl, 14″W	$18.00-22.00
R-968	Star Fish Candleholders, 6″H (ea)	$6.00-8.00
R-974	"S" Shaped Candle Bowl, 22″L	$10.00-12.00
R-975	Running Deer Figurine, 12″L	$12.00-15.00
R-977	Shell Flower Block, 7″W	$12.00-15.00
R-978	Abstract Vase, 10″H	$7.00-9.00
R-979	Abstract Vase, 8″H	$6.00-8.00
R-980	Abstract Vase, 6″H	$4.00-6.00
R-981	Giraffe Figurine, 15″H	$30.00-35.00
R-982	Pelican Vase, 20″H	PND
R-983	Giraffe Planter, 16″L	$30.00-35.00
R-984	Log Planter, 11″L	$8.00-10.00
R-985	Oyster Shell Bowl, 15″W	$10.00-12.00
R-986	Small Basket Vase, 10″H	$15.00-20.00
* R-987	Large Basket Vase, 16″H	$25.00-30.00
R-988	Basket Bowl, 15″L	$12.00-15.00
R-989	Winged Bowl, 12″L	$15.00-18.00
* R-990	Turning Stag, 7″H	$8.00-10.00
* R-991	Standing Stag, 7″H	$8.00-10.00

The following design numbers with the prefix "D" are representative of the d'Este Collection-- previously mentioned in the Finishes Section.

Due to the scarcity of these designs, we cannot yet, attempt to offer a value. Illustrations of these pieces can be seen on pages 3 and 4 of the Royal Haeger by Royal Hickman catalog, as follows:

D-1000	Globe Vase w/swan & cattail, 7″H	
D-1004	Vase, horizontal ribbing, with applied flower stalks, 8″H	
D-1006	Vase, horizontal ribbing, with applied flower stalks, 16″H	
D-1007	Bowl, low with 2 birds, 12½″W	
D-1009	Bowl with applied flowers, 7½″W	
D-1011	Bee Hive Vase with bird on branch, 10½″H	
D-1017	Vase, horizontal ribbing, small neck, 16″H	
D-1018	Vase, horizontal ribbing, small circular base, 9½″W	
D-1019	Vase, round horizontal ribbing, small circular base, 7½″H	
D-1020	Vase, horizontal ribbing with 3 applied lilies, 15″H	
D-1021	Vase, 4 angelfish applied on the side, 15″H	
D-1022	Planter, footed, oblong, with applied branches, 4″H	
D-1023	Vase, horizontal ribbing, applied scattered flowers, 13″H	

A few of these "D" prefix designs surfaced in the Royal Haeger Line, finished in hi-gloss glazes.

* R-1095	Lincoln Ashtray, 7″L	$4.00-6.00
* R-1096	Douglas Ashtray, 7″L	$4.00-6.00
* R-1098	Addams Ashtray, 7″L	$4.00-6.00
R-1115	Candle Bowl, (2 sockets), 13″L	$10.00-12.00
R-1116	Sailfish, 14½″L	$20.00-25.00
R-1119	Horse Planter, 7″H	$12.00-15.00
R-1120	Vase, square, 5½″H	$6.00-8.00
R-1121	Vase, 6″H	$6.00-8.00
* R-1123	Vase, w/Leaves in Relief, 7″H	$7.00-9.00
R-1124	Vase, 8″H	$6.00-8.00
R-1126	Rectangular Concave Bowl, 10½″L	$6.00-8.00
R-1127	Candleholders, 4″L (ea)	$5.00-6.00
R-1129	Angel Fish Ashtray	$6.00-8.00
* R-1130	Single Racing Horse, 9″H	$18.00-20.00
R-1131	Leopard, head, back, tail up, sitting, 8″H	$28.00-30.00
R-1133	Rectangular Bowl, 17″L	$8.00-10.00
R-1134	Ashtray Candleholder, 6½″L (ea)	$5.00-6.00
R-1135	Flower Wall Pocket, 7″W	$6.00-8.00
R-1136	Fish Vase, 6½″H	$10.00-12.00
R-1138	Oval Wraparound Bowl, 6″H	$15.00-18.00
R-1139	Wraparound Vase, 7″H	$10.00-12.00
R-1140	Double Leaf Vase, 8″H	$8.00-10.00
R-1141	Angel Vase, 7″H	$10.00-12.00
R-1143	Swirl Vase, 12½″H	$10.00-15.00
R-1144	Water Lily, Bookend, 5″H, pr.	$18.00-20.00
R-1145	Cig. Box w/cover, 7½″L	$8.00-10.00
* R-1146	Stag Planter, 5½″H	$8.00-10.00
R-1147	Fawn Figurine, 17″L	$20.00-25.00
R-1148	Round Cup Ash Bowl, 6″W	$6.00-8.00
R-1149	Dove Abstract Ashtray, 8″L	$6.00-8.00
R-1150	Abstract Slice Bowl, 8½″L	$6.00-8.00
R-1151	Abstract Animal Bowl, 10″L	$6.00-8.00
R-1152	Golf Club Ashtray, 5″L	$4.00-6.00
R-1154	Abstract Bowl, 17″L	$8.00-10.00

R-1155	Abstract Bird Ash Bowl, 8″L	$6.00-8.00
R-1156	Dbl. Palm Leaf Ashtray, 18½″L	$10.00-12.00
R-1158	Low Pillow Vase, 6″H	$5.00-6.00
R-1159	Vertical Pillow Vase, 8″H	$6.00-8.00
R-1161	Window Box, 13½″L	$7.00-9.00
R-1162	Stepped Wall Pocket, 4½″W	$5.00-7.00
R-1163	Waved Wall Pocket, 4″W	$5.00-7.00
R-1166	Modern Candy Box w/lid, 10″L	$10.00-12.00
R-1168	Large Sailfish Vase, 14½″H	$25.00-30.00
R-1169	Horse & Colt, 11″H	$15.00-20.00
R-1170	Mask Planter, 11″L	$18.00-20.00
R-1171	Double Deer Vase, 12½″H	$20.00-25.00
R-1172	Ashtray, 6½″L	$4.00-6.00
R-1173	Rococo Bowl, 14″L	$7.00-9.00
R-1174	Rococo Candleholder, 6½″L (ea)	$4.00-5.00
R-1175	Wave Candleholder, 5″L (ea)	$4.00-5.00
R-1176	Bowl w/waves, 16″L	$8.00-10.00
R-1177	Neptune Figurine riding sailfish, 20″H	PND
R-1178	Mermaid Figurine, riding sailfish, 20″H	PND
* R-1179	Garden Girl, 14″H	$18.00-22.00
R-1180	Rectangular Fluted Bowl, 15″L	$10.00-12.00
R-1181	Fluted Candleholder, 3½″H (ea)	$5.00-6.00
R-1183	Shell Ash Bowl, 11″L	$5.00-6.00
R-1184	Heart Shaped Ashtray, 7½″L	$6.00-8.00
R-1189	Pine Cone Vase, 9″H	$10.00-12.00
R-1190	Pine Cone Vase, 12″H	$12.00-15.00
R-1191	Sailfish Planter Bowl, 11″L	$18.00-22.00
R-1192	Rectangular Ashtray, 6½″L	$4.00-6.00
R-1195	Abstract Fish Bowl, 14½″L	$8.00-10.00
R-1196	Egg Shaped Div. Bowl, 12″L	$6.00-8.00
R-1197	Treble Candleholders, 3 sockets, 11½″L (ea)	$8.00-10.00
R-1198	Comedy Wall Mask, 11″H	$10.00-12.00
R-1199	Tragedy Wall Mask, 11″H	$10.00-12.00
R-1202	Ashtray w/cig. box/cover combin, 12½″L	$12.00-15.00
R-1203	Twisted Shell Bowl, 17″L	$10.00-12.00
R-1204	Single Leaf Bowl, 9″L	$7.00-9.00
R-1205	Pedestal Bowl w/applied apples, 15¼″L	$20.00-25.00
R-1206	Apple Candleholder, 2½″H (ea)	$6.00-8.00
R-1207	Butterfly Bowl, 14″L	$12.00-15.00
R-1208	Butterfly Candleholder, 6½″L (ea)	$6.00-8.00
R-1210	Cornucopia w/Nude-(Head different from R-426), 7¾″H	$18.00-20.00
R-1211	Leaf Vase, 7½″H	$6.00-8.00
* R-1215	Ballet Vase male, 13½″H	$12.00-15.00
R-1216	Ballet Vase female, 13½″H	$12.00-15.00
R-1218	Swan Flower Bowl, 12″L	$18.00-22.00
R-1220	Gazelle Bowl, 11″L	$15.00-18.00
R-1221	Butterfly Vase, 7½″H	$10.00-12.00
R-1222	Small Classic Vase, 13½″H	$6.00-8.00
R-1223	Large Classic Vase, fan, 18″H	$8.00-10.00
* R-1224	Gypsy Girl, 16½″H	$30.00-35.00
* R-1225	Girl w/2 bowls, 13″L	$20.00-25.00
R-1226	Horse Planter, 8″L	$10.00-12.00
R-1227	Elephant Planter, 8″L	$15.00-18.00
R-1229	Harlequin Planter, 12½″L	$22.00-28.00
R-1230	Dancer Planter, 10½″H	$20.00-25.00
R-1231	St. Francis Figurine, 10½″H	$20.00-25.00
R-1232	St. Francis Bowl, 14″L	$12.00-15.00
* R-1233	Acanthus Console Bowl, 13½″L	$8.00-10.00
R-1234	Acanthus Candleholders, double, 7½″L (ea)	$6.00-8.00
R-1235	Classic Bud Vase, 7½″H	$6.00-8.00
R-1236	3 Bird Bowl, (wings outstretched), 14″L	$18.00-22.00
R-1239	Bronco T.V. Planter, 12″L	$20.00-25.00
* R-1240	Moon Fish Planter Bookend, 10″H (ea)	$15.00-20.00
R-1241	Byzantine Bowl, 14″L,	$10.00-12.00
R-1242	Byzantine Candleholder, 3″H (ea)	$5.00-6.00
R-1245	Oval Executive Ashtray, 15″L	$7.00-9.00
R-1251	Dbl. Ashtray w/cig box/cover combination, 15″L	$15.00-18.00
R-1253	Little Sister, 11½″H	$15.00-18.00
* R-1254	Little Brother, 11½″H	$15.00-18.00
R-1257S	Lorelei (Mermaid), 15″L	$25.00-30.00
* R-1262	Horse Planter, 11″L	$20.00-25.00
* R-1263	Vertical Fluted Vase, 10½″H	$10.00-12.00
R-1264	Vertical Fluted Vase, 13½″H	$12.00-15.00
* R-1265	Colt Figurine, 6″H	$10.00-12.00
R-1266	Helmet Bookend, 9½″H (ea)	$15.00-20.00
R-1267	Lg. Helmet w/wooden base, 18″H	$20.00-25.00
R-1268	"Set" Oval Tropical Console Bowl, 15″L	$10.00-12.00
R-1269	"Set" Tropical Candleholder, 3½″H (ea)	$5.00-6.00
R-1270	Flower Bowl, 15½″L	$10.00-12.00
R-1272	Free Form Ashtray, 11″L	$6.00-8.00
* R-1273	Free Form Ash Bowl, 12″L	$5.00-6.00
R-1275	Diana & Hound, 12″L	$25.00-30.00
R-1283	Fawn Ashtray, 8½″W	$7.00-9.00
* R-1285	Candleholder, 5″H (ea)	$4.00-6.00
R-1286	Vertical Lined Bud Vase, 7½″H	$8.00-10.00
R-1287	Triple Trio Ashtray, 8″W	$4.00-6.00
R-1288	Helmet Ashtray, 9½″L	$10.00-12.00
R-1290	Flower Bowl Candleholder, 5½″L (ea)	$5.00-6.00
R-1293	Acanthus Planter, 11″L	$6.00-8.00
R-1294	Lily Bowl, 12″L	$8.00-10.00
R-1296	Doe & Fawn (lying down), 12″H	$20.00-25.00
R-1301	Giraffe & Young, 13½″H	$20.00-25.00
R-1311	Square Divided Ashtray, 11″W	$6.00-8.00
R-1312	Round Club Ashtray, 5½″L	$5.00-6.00
R-1315	Diamond Ashtray, 9″L	$6.00-8.00
R-1316	Dbl. Leaf Wall Pocket, 11½″W	$10.00-12.00
* R-1318	Upright Cornucopia, 7¾″H	$8.00-10.00
R-1320	Small Flower Bowl, 4½″W	$4.00-6.00
R-1321	Small Flower Ring, 7″W	$7.00-9.00
R-1322	Large Flower Ring, 13″W	$10.00-12.00
R-1324	Horsehead Wall Pocket, 13″L	$12.00-15.00
R-1325	Doe Head Wall Pocket, 10″H	$10.00-12.00
R-1327	Ruching Ashtray, 13″L	$5.00-7.00
R-1328	Dbl. Ruching Ashtray, 13½″L	$10.00-12.00
R-1331	Greyhound Planter, 12″L	$18.00-20.00
R-1332	Seagull Fish Bowl, 14″H	$25.00-30.00
R-1333	Double Vase, 7½″H	$8.00-10.00
R-1335	Winged Bowl, 18½″L	$8.00-12.00
R-1336	Winged Vase, 10½″H	$10.00-12.00
R-1336	Winged Vase, 7½″H	$6.00-8.00
R-1337	Double Swirl Bowl, 11″L	$8.00-10.00
R-1338	Modern Bowl, 13″L	$6.00-8.00
R-1339	Modern Candleholder, 5″L (ea)	$5.00-6.00
R-1340	Candlebowl, 3 sockets, 12″L	$10.00-12.00
R-1345	Cornucopia Planter, 9½″L	$6.00-8.00
R-1346	Ridged Ashtray, 8″L	$6.00-8.00
R-1347	Free Form Cig. Box Ashtray, 11½″L	$8.00-10.00
R-1348	Upright Cornucopia, 8″H	$6.00-8.00
R-1349	Horse Ashtray, 11″L	$18.00-20.00
* R-1351	Fawn Planter, 17″L	$10.00-15.00
R-1352	Duck Vase, 7½″H	$15.00-18.00
R-1353	Leaf Edged Console Bowl, 11″L	$8.00-10.00
* R-1354	Leaf Edged Candleholder, 3″H (ea)	$4.00-5.00
R-1356	Dented Flatsided Bowl, 10½″H	$10.00-12.00
R-1357	Square Ridged Ashtray, 6″W	$4.00-6.00
R-1359	Pear Shaped Ashtray, 7″L	$7.00-9.00

R-1360	Shell Bowl, 15"L	$8.00-10.00
R-1363	Double Heart Ashtray, 9"L	$6.00-8.00
* R-1364	Rococo Bookend, 6"H(pr)	$18.00-20.00
R-1365	Horsehead Figurine or Bookend, 7"H (ea)	$12.00-15.00
R-1366	Bridge Table Ashtray Floor Smoker, w/wrought iron stand, 29½"H	$15.00-18.00
R-1368	Mare & Foal, lying down, 9"H	$20.00-25.00
R-1369	Stag Cig. Box & Ashtray Combination, 6"H	$12.00-15.00
R-1370	Treble Lily Vase, 10½"H	$15.00-20.00
* R-1375	Wicker Basket, 9"H	$8.00-10.00
R-1376	Rectangular Ashtray, 12½"L	$5.00-6.00
R-1377	Modern Triple Vase, 12"H	$10.00-15.00
R-1378	Free Form Floor Ashtray, w/wrought iron stand, 26"H	$15.00-18.00
R-1381	Square Vase, side handles, 14"H	$8.00-10.00
R-1382	Raised Leaf Ashtray, 8"L	$4.00-6.00
R-1387	Ashtray Bowl, 4"H	$6.00-8.00
R-1388	Rectangular Bowl w/4 feet, 14"L	$15.00-20.00
R-1391	Square Ashtray w/4 feet, 6"L	$4.00-6.00
R-1392	Straight Urn Vase, 16"H	$8.00-10.00
R-1393	Bottle Vase, cascade, 13½"H	$6.00-8.00
R-1394	Bottle Vase, 16"H	$6.00-8.00
R-1396	Boxer (dog) Figurine, 11"L	$20.00-22.00
R-1397	Haeger's Royal Susan, (without center cover), 18"W	$20.00-25.00
R-1398SC	Haeger's Royal Susan, complete, side dishes & center bowl w/cover, 18"W	$25.00-30.00
R-1399	Boxer (dog) Figurine Ashtray, 13"L	$20.00-25.00
R-1400	Fluted Bowl, 6"H	$6.00-8.00
R-1401	Large Swan Vase, 12½"H	$15.00-18.00
R-1402	Large Bird Bowl, 16½"L	$18.00-20.00
R-1403	Rectangular Ashtray, 8"L	$4.00-6.00
R-1404	Colt Figurine, 5½"H	$12.00-15.00
R-1405	Mare Figurine, 7½"H	$15.00-18.00
R-1406	Fluted Vase, 12"H	$8.00-10.00
R-1407	Thunder & Lightning Figurine (3 horses), 17½"H	PND
R-1408	Sands of Time Ashtray, 12"L	$7.00-9.00
R-1410	Tempo Bowl, 9½"L	$6.00-8.00
R-1411	Lined Bowl, 10"L	$6.00-8.00
R-1412	Triangular Candy Bowl, 10½"W	$8.00-10.00
R-1413	Round Bowl, 10½"W	$8.00-10.00
R-1414	Round Candleholder, 5"W(ea)	$5.00-7.00
R-1415	Oblong Bowl, 12"L	$8.00-10.00
R-1416	Oblong Planter w/stand, 14"L	$10.00-12.00
R-1417	Pie Crust Ashtray, w/wrought iron stand, 4"W	$8.00-10.00
R-1421	Single Handled Bowl, 15"L	$8.00-10.00
R-1424	Ashtray Cig. Tray, 10½"L	$8.00-10.00
R-1428	Square Ashtray, 10½"W	$8.00-10.00
R-1429	Square Ashtray, 8½"W	$6.00-8.00
R-1430	Square Ashtray, 6½"W	$5.00-6.00
R-1431	Square Ashtray, 4½"W	$4.00-5.00
R-1433	Candy Box on 3 ball feet, 10"L	$8.00-10.00
R-1433B	Bowl on Feet, 10"L	$8.00-10.00
R-1434	Modern Rose Bowl on 3 ball feet, 15"L	$10.00-12.00
R-1436	Split Cir. Ashtray & Cig Box Comb, 9½"L	$12.00-15.00
R-1437	Modern Triple Planter, 13½"W	$8.00-10.00
R-1438	Ash Bowl & Pipe Stand, 8"L	$6.00-8.00
R-1440	Poodle Figurine, 8"H	$20.00-22.00
R-1441	Poodle Ashtray, 12"L	$20.00-25.00
R-1442	Standing Cocker Figurine, 7½"H	$20.00-22.00
R-1443	Standing Cocker Ashtray, 12"L	$20.00-25.00
R-1445	Vertical Ribbed Vase, 12"H	$10.00-12.00
R-1446	Basket Planter, 9"H	$8.00-10.00
R-1448	Modern Peacock Vase, 15"H	$20.00-22.00
R-1449	Large Rose Bowl on 3 ball feet, 15"L	$10.00-12.00
R-1450	Fish Vase, 4"H	$6.00-8.00
R-1451	Rooster Vase, 4"H	$6.00-8.00
R-1452	Oblong Bowl, 5½"L	$4.00-6.00
R-1453	Round Urn, 4"H	$4.00-6.00
R-1454	Leaf Vase, 4"H	$4.00-6.00
* R-1455	Stag Vase, 4½"H	$6.00-8.00
R-1456	Bow-Tie Vase, 3"H	$5.00-6.00
R-1457	Horsehead Vase, 4"H	$6.00-8.00
R-1458	Globe Vase, 4½H	$4.00-6.00
R-1460	Double Leaf Vase, 11"H	$6.00-8.00
R-1462	Wheelbarrow Planter, 10"L	$8.00-10.00
R-1465	Flying Duck Vase, 14"H	$20.00-25.00
R-1466	Bridge Table Ashtray Floor Smoker w/wrought iron stand, 27"H	$15.00-20.00
R-1467	Rippled Oval Console Bowl, 12½"L	$10.00-12.00
R-1468	Singing Bird, 4"H	$6.00-8.00
R-1469	Feeding Bird, 3½"H	$6.00-8.00
R-1470	Square Rippled Ashtray, 7½"W	$6.00-8.00
R-1471	Abstract Fish Ashtray, 13"L	$8.00-10.00
R-1472	Freedom Ashtray, 11"L	$6.00-8.00
R-1473	Modern Ashtray, 9"L	$4.00-6.00
R-1474	Round Chinese Bell Shaped Bowl, 6¾"L	$4.00-6.00
R-1475	Square Chinese Bell Shaped Bowl, 5"H	$4.00-6.00
R-1476	Rectangular Footed Bowl, 15"L	$8.00-10.00
R-1477	Modern Bowl, 14"L	$7.00-9.00
R-1478	Oval Footed Empire Bowl, 10"L	$6.00-8.00
R-1479	Classic Urn Vase, 12"H	$8.00-10.00
R-1480	Rectangular Cigarette Box, 6½"L	$6.00-8.00
R-1481	Oval Ashtray, 8"L	$4.00-6.00
R-1482	Rectangular Ashtray (set of 3), 4½"L	$8.00-10.00
	"set", 5"L	$4.00-6.00
	"set", 6"L	$7.00-9.00
R-1483	Advertising Soap Dish "1907-1957", Weise's 50th, 8"L	$6.00-8.00
R-1485	Round Ashtray, 8"W	$4.00-6.00
R-1486	Round Candy Box & Cover, 8"H	$8.00-10.00
R-1487	Three Sided Ash Bowls (nest), 4½"L	$4.00-6.00
	"set", 5½"L	$4.00-6.00
	"set", 6"L	$4.00-6.00
R-1490	Three Legged Vase, 18"H	$8.00-10.00
R-1491	Three Legged Vase, 12"H	$7.00-9.00
R-1492	Three Legged Vase, 10"H	$6.00-8.00
R-1493	Three Legged Candleholder, 4"H (ea)	$4.00-6.00
R-1494	Three Legged Low Bowl, 3"H	$6.00-8.00
R-1495	Contemporary Vase, 15"H	$8.00-10.00
R-1496	Contemporary Low Bow, 15"L	$6.00-8.00
R-1497	Contemporary Candleholder, 4"H(ea)	$4.00-6.00
R-1498	Ruffled Top Vase, 13½"H	$8.00-10.00
R-1499	Ruffled Top Vase, 7½"H	$7.00-9.00
R-1500	Modern Double Loop Vase, 8"H	$8.00-10.00

Schroeder's Antiques Price Guide

Schroeder's Antiques Price Guide has climbed its way to the top in a field already supplied with several well-established publications! The word is out, *Schroeder's Price Guide* is the best buy at any price. Over 500 categories are covered, with more than 50,000 listings. But it's not volume alone that makes Schroeder's the unique guide it is recognized to be. From ABC Plates to Zsolnay, if it merits the interest of today's collector, you'll find it in Schroeder's. Each subject is represented with histories and background information. In addition, hundreds of sharp original photos are used each year to illustrate not only the rare and the unusual, but the everyday "fun-type" collectibles as well -- not postage stamp pictures, but large close-up shots that show important details clearly.

Each edition is completely re-typeset from all new sources. We have not and will not simply change prices in each new edition. All new copy and all new illustrations make Schroeder's THE price guide on antiques and collectibles.

The writing and researching team behind this giant is proportionately large. It is backed by a staff of more than seventy of Collector Books' finest authors, as well as a board of advisors made up of well-known antique authorities and the country's top dealers, all specialists in their fields. Accuracy is their primary aim. Prices are gathered over the entire year previous to publication, from ads and personal contacts. Then each category is thoroughly checked to spot inconsistencies, listings that may not be entirely reflective of actual market dealings, and lines too vague to be of merit. Only the best of the lot remains for publication. You'll find *Schroeder's Antiques Price Guide* the one to buy for factual information and quality.

No dealer, collector or investor can afford not to own this book. It is available from your favorite bookseller or antiques dealer at the low price of $12.95. If you are unable to find this price guide in your area, it's available from Collector Books, P. O. Box 3009, Paducah, KY 42001 at $12.95 plus $2.00 for postage and handling.

8½ x 11, 608 Pages $12.95